D1711235

THE PRESIDENT
FROM TEXAS:

LYNDON
BAINES
JOHNSON

THE PRESIDENT FROM TEXAS:

LYNDON BAINES JOHNSON

by Dudley Lynch

illustrated with photographs

THOMAS Y. CROWELL COMPANY • NEW YORK

For
Kim and Mendy
(who would have charmed
him)

Photos 1–12, 14, 16, 18–20 courtesy of the Lyndon Baines Johnson
Library. Photos 13, 15, 17 from United Press International, Inc.

Designed by Helga Maass
Manufactured in the United States of America

Library of Congress Cataloging in Publication Data

Lynch, Dudley M   1940–
    The President from Texas: Lyndon Baines Johnson.

    SUMMARY: A biography of the Texas Senator who became thirty-
sixth President of the United States.

    1. Johnson, Lyndon Baines, Pres. U. S., 1908–1973—Juv. lit.
[1. Johnson, Lyndon Baines, Pres. U. S., 1908–1973.   2.   Presidents]
I.   Title.
E847.L96   973.923′092′4 [B] [92]   74–26817
ISBN 0–690–00627–6

1   2   3   4   5   6   7   8   9   10

Contents

Illustrations follow page 84

Chapter 1

BIRTH OF A SENATOR

For Sam Ealy Johnson, Jr., Lyndon's father, early rising was a habit, all right, but it was more than that. A matter of pride, perhaps. He was up stretching, scratching, sorting out his day, putting all of his plans together before the sun had appeared each morning. Even in the summer, when the days started so early, he was up, bustling around before the buzzards had yet to stir a stiffened wing in the twisted live oak trees of central Texas.

Each morning, just as he had done the morning before, Sam rose from his bed, dressed quickly, and made himself a fire. Then he lit the kerosene lamp in the kitchen of the Johnsons' rambling country cottage. With his whiskers always black and heavy, he used an ivory-handled straight razor to shave, being careful not to nick himself in the lamp's glow. It was a gaunt face that he saw each time in his tiny mirror. Gaunt, with a finely etched mouth, a hairline that was rising steadily with the years, and rigid outcroppings for cheekbones.

After he finished shaving, he invariably ate a breakfast of fried or scrambled eggs, slices of tangy smoked ham, and big piles of pan-browned potatoes. Usually, since early rising was a man's task, Johnson ate breakfast alone. But today, there had been no eggs cooked, and Sam hadn't shaved. The lamps had burned brightly all night, and he hadn't slept, either. For in the living room-bedroom of their white frame cabin, lying in their four-poster bed, Rebekah Baines Johnson was about to give birth. It would be—and Sam was proud of the fact—the Johnsons' first baby.

Mrs. Johnson, a cultured woman of poetry and letters, would remember this sunrise vividly. "Now the light came in from the east," she wrote. It brought a deep stillness, "a stillness so profound and so pervasive that it seemed as if the earth itself were listening."

Her husband, to be blunt about it, would have liked to have heard the sound of a horse and buggy. How many times had he stepped outside and looked up and down in vain for the doctor? The air was already warming on this humid August day, and there was no sign and no sound of Dr. John Blanton of Buda, whipping his buggy from the southeast. The night before, they had summoned a German midwife, just in case Doc Blanton was late. As his young wife's labor pains grew stronger and stronger, Johnson said, "It's up to you, Mrs. Lindig."

The baby came shortly after daybreak, and the doctor just after that. The doctor bounced the red-faced infant in his hands, carefully examining the huge ears, smooth cheeks, and the tiny frown. "Ten pounds, I'd say," Blanton guessed finally. The sleeping little boy looked healthy, and Rebekah Johnson, who had a broad face and rosy lips, thought that he more nearly favored his father, Little Sam.

With the new baby born, Sam Johnson, Jr. could control his joy no longer. Riding his gray horse, Fritz, he galloped off to the home of his parents, Sam and Eliza Johnson, who lived a quarter of a mile away. Then he sped on to his sister's, bearing the news. By late afternoon, just about everyone in Gillespie and Blanco counties knew that the Sam Johnsons had a son. If they hadn't heard the announcement from Little Sam, they had heard it from his father, Big Sam. Sam Johnson, Sr. had also mounted his horse and rode far. The news he gave out was, "A United States senator was born today—my grandson!"

It was not Big Sam's first grandchild; he had four others. But on this Thursday—August 27, 1908—Big Sam Johnson seemed to think that a child of unusual promise had been born. Why not a U.S. senator?

But first, the new Johnson baby needed a name.

It wasn't Rebekah Johnson's idea to call him "Baby" for the first three months of his life, but every time she suggested a name, her husband objected. One morning, as Johnson sat putting on his boots by the fireplace, she said it was time that their baby had a name. Her tone said that she meant business. This time, she ordered Sam Johnson, Jr. to suggest names and *she*, Rebekah Johnson, was going to be the judge.

So he proposed "Clarence," thinking of his favorite brother-in-law.

"That won't do," she snapped peevishly.

"Dayton," he said, for Dayton Moses, the district attorney.

She shook her head again.

"Linden," he came back, referring to his lawyer friend, W. C. Linden.

That seemed to bring a sparkle to the eyes of the pretty blonde woman, but she insisted, "Only if I may spell it as I like."

By now her husband was hungry and cross. "Spell it any

way you want," Johnson retorted. So Mrs. Johnson decided it would be "Lyndon" for the first name and "Baines," her family's name, for the middle. Lyndon Baines Johnson. His grandfather wrote in a letter to little Lyndon's Aunt Lucie, "I expect him to be United States senator before he is forty."

The roots of politics pushed deep into the family background of Lyndon Baines Johnson.

While campaigning in Georgia for the Kennedy-Johnson Democratic ticket of 1960, Lyndon reminded a political rally crowd that "my grandfather, Jesse Johnson, was elected sheriff of Henry County." Thus it was in Georgia, Lyndon added, that "the Johnson family got its start in politics."

He was half right. Jesse Johnson was his *great*-grandfather, not his grandfather. But Lyndon was correct in advancing the name of Jesse Johnson as the starting point. In 1846, at the age of fifty-one, it was a restless Jesse who moved an entourage that included his wife, Lucy Webb, their youngest children, the five children of a widower son, and the family slaves to Texas by covered wagon.

The baby of the family was eight-year-old Samuel Ealy Johnson, Lyndon's "Grandpaw." Eleven years after the Johnsons staked out their farm at Lockhart, in south-central Texas, Sam's father died, and a year later, his mother. Sam and brother Jesse Thomas (Tom), two years older, pushed on to the Hill Country, fifty miles west, seeking a new life. East of Fredericksburg, they built a log cabin and entered the cattle-trading business.

Though the Civil War interrupted briefly, Sam acquired a wife, Eliza Bunton, and Tom acquired a 320-acre ranch in Blanco County, along the Pedernales River. Using the ranch as a base of operations, the brothers organized trail drives to the railroads in Kansas, and their business thrived. But in 1871, the demand for beef dropped, and with no market Sam and Tom were forced to winter their herds in Kansas. Many cattle died, and the Johnson brothers were ruined as cattle traders.

Tom died in 1877. Sam moved to Buda in neighboring Hays County, where Sam Ealy, Jr. was born in October, 1877.

When Sam, Jr. was twelve, Big Sam, as his father was called, moved the family west to a farm near Johnson City. Lyndon always said that Johnson City was named after his grandfather. Actually, the dusty little town was named after its founder, James Polk Johnson, nephew of Big Sam.

At age eighteen, Little Sam began to teach school. After two years in the classroom, he tried farming. In 1905, at age twenty-six, he won a seat in the Texas legislature, where he was known as a "straight-shootin' " lawmaker with a "cussed streak of independence." In 1907, he won another two-year term.

In August of that year, the thirty-year-old Johnson married twenty-six-year-old Rebekah Baines. She was the daughter of Joseph Wilson Baines of Blanco, a former legislator, a lawyer and a newspaper editor. Rebekah was bright and well-read. Later, one Blanco banker would say, "That's where Lyndon got his brains." Except for her father, she came from a family of preachers and the wives of preachers.

Her grandfather, the Rev. George Washington Baines, Sr., had presided over Baylor College for two years during the Civil War. Earlier, the Rev. Baines had preached for the Huntsville, Texas, Baptist Church, where the legendary Texas hero Sam Houston attended.

On the Johnson side, the relatives of Lyndon's grandmother, Eliza Bunton Johnson, stood out. Grandmaw Johnson was a niece of John Wheeler Bunton, in 1836 one of the fifty-nine signers of the Texas Declaration of Independence. Bunton also served in the first Congress of the Republic of Texas. And Eliza Johnson had two famous cousins: Governor Joseph Desha of Kentucky and Mary Desha, who was a co-founder of the Daughters of the American Revolution.

Lyndon's maternal grandfather, Joseph Baines, in addition to being a legislator in Arkansas and Texas, had served Texas in the 1880s as Secretary of State. Lyndon's father, Little Sam, had many months to go as a legislator at the time of his son's birth. Later, starting in 1918, Little Sam campaigned again and again, winning every time. He remained in the Texas legislature until 1925.

These forces of family ties, family interests, and family positions came to bear strongly on little Lyndon. His mother, completely dedicated to her son, taught him his alphabet by the time he was two. At the age of three, according to Rebekah Johnson, Lyndon knew "all the Mother Goose rhymes." Not long after his fourth birthday, he was reading to his Grandpaw Johnson and to his teacher, Miss Kate Deadrich, who agreed to let him start school early.

When not at school, Lyndon was often hiding in the bedroom behind the Johnsons' front porch. His ear to the screen, he could overhear conversations between his father and the many visitors to the Johnson place. Conversations about running for office. About political favors. About political pressures and about political strategies.

These long, often lively talks, sometimes between only two persons and sometimes among many, were always about Democratic party politics—not Republican party politics or any other party's. During Lyndon's boyhood days, and for most of his life, Texas was a one-party state. It wasn't until he became President that the Republicans began to elect a few Texas officials, finally overcoming the stigma placed against the party by the Republican-sponsored carpetbagging era that followed the American Civil War in the South.

Lyndon quickly demonstrated that he didn't just tolerate all of the political talk and activity around him. He *enjoyed* it. That became clear one Fourth of July when the governor of Texas came to Johnson City and, after making a speech, went on to the Johnsons' house.

For the evening meal, Rebekah Johnson banished Lyndon and his sisters, Rebekah and Josefa, who were younger than he, to the kitchen. Before long, she was wondering why she hadn't also banished Lucie Price, her sister-in-law. Lucie was acting strangely. Several times she sat upright, suddenly reaching for a piece of chicken.

Later, Mrs. Johnson learned the truth.

"Oh, that was Lyndon," Lucie explained sheepishly. "He wanted to hear the political talk, so I let him hide under the tablecloth. I told him to pinch me whenever he got hungry and I'd hand him a piece of chicken."

One turn of the crank and the Model T Ford's engine caught, chugging. The family's hounds, tied to a nearby oak tree, howled mournfully, but Lyndon was too excited, too expectant to notice. He was hitting the campaign trail again with his dad, who was politicking, running for the Texas Legislature.

On the front porch, Rebekah Johnson wiped her hands on a flowery apron as she watched them leave. She smiled, thrusting out her firm chin, shaking her head. She didn't care for all the howdying, handshaking, and glad-handing that politics required. Some people said she was aloof, but she credited it simply to a little dignity, maybe even a little more sense.

Lyndon heard his dad call, "Okay, son, here's what we're gonna do for today." Not wanting to miss a word, the young campaigner strained toward his father, ears tingling, as they drove on to Johnson City.

They campaigned all that summer of 1920, traveling first to one and then to another of the four counties that made up the 89th District. Lyndon liked to watch his dad. Little Sam was handsome, with hair as black as a midnight without a moon. Because he was so tall—six feet, two inches—he usually towered above any crowd. He moved easily among people, asking how the crops were coming and when the new baby was due. He loved people.

With summer lengthening, Lyndon realized that he was learning a lot about two things: the countryside around his daddy's farm and the landscape of Texas politics.

Several times that summer, they drove past Junction School, where he had just finished the seventh grade. Next year, he would go to Stonewall School, a two-mile ride by donkey. Later, he would transfer to Albert School and ride a horse.

Riding along in his dad's car, one foot propped up on the dash, Lyndon could gaze at the neighboring hills, faint and hazed at mid-day. But as the shadows lengthened, the hills were so sharp that Lyndon could practically count the leaves on the juniper, live oak and white oak trees, and count the grass clumps below.

This was the Texas Hill Country, a kingdom of rolling crags and canyons, tree-lined rivers and pleasant valleys. The Hill Country began just west of Austin, the state capital, and ran west for about a hundred miles, covering forty counties. With little top soil and an ocean of rocks in any direction, it could be a harsh land, but Lyndon loved it. The area he loved most was close to his father's farm, along the Pedernales River, under the canopies that were formed by the broad-limbed trees.

As they drove along one afternoon late in the campaign, Lyndon called out to his father, "Buzzards circlin' up ahead."

Little Sam's reply startled Lyndon. "They ain't the only buzzards in Texas." He spat angrily. Lyndon guessed the German issue was troubling his father. The subject came up every time they stopped to visit in the heavily German Fredericksburg area, in the western part of the 89th District. In that part of the Hill Country, Sam Johnson, Jr. was a hero.

Lyndon knew the whole story. He knew that his father had been viciously maligned that winter in a special session of the legislature because he had dared to defend Texas citizens with German backgrounds. At issue was a bill that would have permitted any Texan to arrest any person he thought was "disloyal." Johnson fought that idea successfully, but he wasn't able to keep the legislature from passing a bill setting a prison term for anyone caught uttering a disloyal expression. The bill was aimed mostly at the Germans in the Hill Country, who had been just as loyal to the U.S. during World War I as anyone else.

The Fredericksburg newspaper had praised Johnson for fighting the bill. The German farmers praised him, too. When the ballots were counted, Sam Johnson was an easy winner. The county fair speeches and the picnics, the traveling from town to town and farm to farm, the long, dusty days and the warm, starry nights—it all had paid off, again.

That winter, when Sam Johnson traveled to Austin to the

legislature, son Lyndon often went with him. Before long, young Lyndon knew every nook and cranny of the marble Texas statehouse just about as well as he knew the hiding places along the banks of the Pedernales. He made lots of friends, particularly among the page boys.

The legislators found it fascinating to watch Sam Johnson and his son. Usually, Sam's five-gallon hat was resting on top of the papers on his desk, and he often wore a flower in his lapel. Standing at his daddy's side, listening to the speeches and watching the lawmakers operate, Lyndon looked just like his father. He walked and talked like his father. Many of the legislators suspected that someday young Lyndon would be a politician himself, maybe a good one.

Today was May 4, 1924, and a crowd had gathered on the second floor of the stone-walled Johnson City High School. With so many parents and classmates attending, fifteen-year-old Lyndon Johnson cleared his throat nervously. Ten-year-old Sam Houston Johnson and his friend Clem Davis, the preacher's son, straightened in their seats. All eyes were now on the lanky, black-haired youth who was about to speak.

There were six graduates in all, four of them girls. Poor John Dollahite, shy with the girls, had had no chance. With Margaret, Georgia, Louise and Kittie Clyde voting for him, Lyndon had won the class presidency. But grades, not votes, were the reason why Lyndon was the Commencement Day speaker. He was the class valedictorian, with the best grades of the class of '24.

". . . and fellow graduates," Lyndon was soon intoning.

It was obvious that the theme of his speech was ambition. Surely, that came as no surprise to anyone who knew the speaker.

It wouldn't have surprised Anna Itz, one of Lyndon's former classmates. One day under a pecan tree during a recess at Albert School, Lyndon had confided to Anna, "Someday I'm going to be President of the United States."

Johnson City's only barber, on the other hand, remembered well the time when Lyndon, about ten, decided to take a front-page newspaper ad promoting his shoeshine business. The ad had angered Lyndon's dad. As a politician, he didn't think it wise for the voters to know his son worked, even part-time, as a bootblack.

Johnny Casparis, son of the Casparis Cafe owner, wasn't surprised. He and Lyndon had teamed that year in the district debate competition at San Marcos. Lyndon had worked himself into an excited frenzy, and when they lost, he actually had become ill from the disappointment.

Despite his mother's speech lessons, Lyndon still mumbled occasionally, but his enthusiasm removed the force of the handicap. He was about the tallest person in the room. With those long arms and lanky legs, he could stretch a mile, and that had made him a natural first baseman. During track season, he had thrown the discus.

Lyndon was saying that everybody should have a special goal in life. That was what ambition, he suggested, was all about. "Just take my brother," he said, glancing at Sam Houston, who suddenly paled, wondering what his big brother was up to. He found out quickly.

"Somebody once asked Sam Houston what he wanted to be," said Lyndon, pausing for effect, "and he replied, 'I want to be Grandmaw's girl and a Baptist preacher.' "

The crowd roared, just as Lyndon knew they would. But young Sam, seeing nothing funny in the story, fled tearfully from the building, and it was years before he fully appreciated the humor.

Later, Lyndon occasionally used that story during his campaigns for Congress. In May, 1924, however, Congress was not in his thoughts—or college. The youngest graduate in the history of Johnson City High School was through with school forever, he said bluntly. No sooner was he handed his high school diploma than he began to think seriously about California. The idea also intrigued the Crider brothers, Otho Summy and his brother, and Payne Roundtree. Within a few days, Lyndon had convinced all of them to join him.

They were going to pool their money, buy a car, and drive 1,400 miles to the Pacific Ocean.

Chapter 2

TRAINING GROUND

He was an inch or two taller and several pounds skinnier than before he left, and he was weary and homesick. With only a few more miles to Johnson City, Lyndon could imagine how his grandmother's quilt looked as it lay neatly folded at the foot of his bed. He had been gone nearly two years.

On that July day in '24, he had left without saying a single goodbye. And he hadn't written many letters. Just a few notes to say that the Johnson City gang was picking grapes, washing dishes, waiting tables. One letter said they had finally split up in the Imperial Valley. He hadn't explained why, but he knew that his parents were quick enough, shrewd enough, to figure it out. And they were. They had guessed correctly that the boys were hungry and broke.

Rather than come home, he had hitchhiked to Los Angeles, where he operated an elevator and clerked in a law firm. "I imagine Lyndon was principally motivated by a sense of adventure," his brother Sam Houston said years later. "He just wanted to roam somewhere else."

Now, he was hitchhiking home. He suspected that the

law-clerking was the only part of his adventure that his mother had approved of. He was equally sure that Rebekah Johnson was immediately going to ask, "Well, are you about ready to settle down and go off to college?"

He'd know soon.

There was the Casparis Cafe. The sign made him hungry for a bowl of Mexican T-bone. That's what he had called the Casparises' red-pepper chili since back before he could remember. And Lyndon knew that whatever his mother said, he wasn't about to go off to college.

It wasn't Lyndon's mother who kept mentioning college. It was Sam Ealy Johnson, Jr. To his stubborn son, Sam Johnson said, "It's fine to be satisfied with the simple things. A man who is satisfied to be a laborer will never have much on his mind. Of course, he really won't need much." Lyndon agreed. A paycheck, a bed, and some entertainment occasionally.

The remainder of 1926 Lyndon worked as a dollar-a-day driver for the county road crew. Occasionally, he got into fights in Fredericksburg, the German town about thirty miles to the west. Many of its citizens didn't understand English, and it was easy to start a Saturday night misunderstanding. After one fist fight, Lyndon's father advised, "Next time you want to be noticed, try some other way." Through her tears, his mother said, "To think that my eldest born should turn out like this."

That summer, Lyndon joined a church, the Disciples of Christ. But religion didn't reduce his enthusiasm for a good fight. It had little effect on his interest in trading the cab of his road-crew truck for a college classroom desk, either.

What did, finally?

The weather. After two years in sunny Southern California, Lyndon had forgotten Hill Country winters. In late fall, the northers swept in, bringing frigid winds that turned his hands the color of raw mutton. One blustery February day in 1927, after spending twelve straight hours on the road gang, Lyndon startled his mother and father with an unexpected announcement: "I'm ready to start working with my brain. If you can get me into San Marcos, I'm ready to go."

He'd had enough.

Southwest Texas State College at San Marcos was not a likely school for a future President of the United States. It wasn't even the region's most prestigious college, an honor that went to the state university at Austin, fifty miles away. Southwest Texas State College was certainly not Harvard (which produced both Adamses, both Roosevelts, and John F. Kennedy), or Princeton (Madison and Wilson), or William and Mary (Jefferson, Monroe, and Tyler). It was, simply, a good college for a small-town Texas teen-ager with more ambition than cash.

Lyndon lived in a number of boardinghouses, paying about $30 a month for food and lodging. It was at one such rooming place, Mrs. Gates' house on Edward Gary Street, where he took his meals, that he established his reputation for his "boardinghouse reach." Mrs. Gates, wide and matronly, would thunder, "You can eat all you want, but one foot stays on the floor at all times!" With his long scoop-shovel arms, Lyndon quickly discovered that he could lean down the boardinghouse table and spear a surplus of pork chops deftly—always keeping one foot on the floor.

Two years as a common laborer hadn't dulled Lyndon's political instincts—his "feel" for people and power developed by all those years as his father's understudy. A cousin, Ava

Johnson, remembers some of Lyndon's advice during a walk across the campus. "The first thing you want to do is to know people—and don't play sandlot ball," Lyndon spouted. "Play in the big leagues. Get to know the first team."

At Southwest Texas State, that meant befriending the college president, Dr. Cecil Evans, an idea that terrified Ava. "I wouldn't dare to go up to President Evans' office," she whispered.

"That's where you want to start," Lyndon snapped.

Within a few weeks, operating on this philosophy, Lyndon got himself promoted three times in his student jobs. The third time was to a post as assistant to President Evans' personal secretary, Tom Nichols. Mostly, this involved carrying messages from and to the president's office, since there was no campus-wide telephone system. But Lyndon viewed the job as more than a mere messenger boy's.

Department heads soon suspected that Lyndon had been given considerable powers and responsibilities. They often made their appointments with Evans through him. And Evans, in turn, did widen Lyndon's duties. He began to travel with the college president to the legislature to lobby on education matters. Before long, he was also writing reports to state officials and answering some of Evans' correspondence.

"Lyndon," Evans told him years later, "you hadn't been in my office a month before I could hardly tell who was president of the school—you or me."

A secretive group of athletes known as the Black Stars controlled campus politics, and Lyndon quickly sized up prospects there, too. At first, he tried to join the Black Stars, arguing that his job in the president's office would be valuable to the club even though he wasn't an athlete. But a single Black Star blackballed him during the membership vote because of jealousy over a girl friend. Thus affronted, Lyndon formed his own club, the White Stars.

It took but one election for the White Stars to win control of campus politics. They planned cleverly and organized well, and no one organized with more skill than Lyndon. Some students thought he was ruthless. "Every action was calculated to advance his career," fussed one classmate—and Lyndon would probably have been the last to deny it.

In the winter of 1930, the White Stars nominated Willard Deason, one of Lyndon's close friends, for president of the senior class. He was running against a popular Black Star candidate, Dick Spinn, an athlete. The night before the vote, the White Stars assembled with grim faces. Their talks with individual seniors indicated that Deason was about fifteen votes short. Discouraged at the tally, most of the youths quit and went to bed. But not Lyndon.

"When ordinary men were ready to give up, that's when Lyndon was just beginning," Deason later commented. All night long, Lyndon telephoned the girls and visited the boys among the ninety seniors. Each time, the sleepy student received "the Johnson treatment," intended to win backing for Deason. And it worked, for the next day Deason won by eight votes.

Lyndon's political skills pleased no one more than H. M. Greene, professor of government. Greene was a maverick. He liked to read Henry David Thoreau and he liked to be alone in the wilds: to think, to reflect, to hear nature out. He loved his students, and he loved politics. He was not only Lyndon's government teacher but he was also Lyndon's debate coach.

Lyndon's debate partner was a student named Elmer Graham. They paired well, though Graham often complained that Lyndon made him do all the work. Lyndon had no interest in organizing materials, but he was masterful in taking an argument by the opposing college team and demolishing it. Forcefully.

Greene said that the two most heated antagonists he ever taught were Lyndon Johnson and a student named Henry Kyle. As luck would have it, they were both in the same class. When measured by Kyle's decidedly conservative views, Lyndon's were liberal. Says Greene, "I never saw Lyndon 'outdone' by a student, though Henry Kyle often *pushed* him to his best."

Lyndon's government teacher and debate coach had one recurring bit of advice to give him: "Son, if I were headed for the political arena, I would bear in mind that the United States Senate is one spot where a man of integrity has a real opportunity to serve his country."

But Lyndon wasn't sure whether he wanted to pursue politics or teaching. During the 1928-29 term, he had served as a principal in Cotulla, Texas. At age twenty, he was placed in charge of the Welhausen Ward School, where he supervised five teachers, taught the sixth and seventh grade classes, and helped the janitor manage the physical plant. All of the school's students were Mexican-Americans. They were poor, spoke little or no English, and were difficult to teach. But Lyndon did not dodge the challenge. Quickly convinced that the children must learn English to succeed in a culture dominated by English-speaking people, he insisted that this language be spoken on the school campus. He insisted that his teachers supervise the children constantly, and he insisted that his students work, and work hard. If they failed to study, they were likely to be punished. Lyndon organized many activities —debates, regular assemblies, athletic field days, out-of-town trips—that the youngsters had never participated in before, and when, at the end of the school term, he decided to return to college, everyone in Cotulla spoke highly of his achievements as a principal. The $125 monthly salary, moreover, had replenished his school funds, and he returned to San Marcos for his junior and senior years. By the time of his graduation, in August of 1930, his uncle, George Desha Johnson, had gotten him a contract to teach in the Houston, Texas, public schools as soon as there was a vacancy.

But even then, as Lyndon confided one day to a friend, "I don't know whether I want to stay in teaching or not. I think I would like to get into politics."

He was a magnet for politicians and political dealings. He demonstrated that anew during the summer of 1930. This was at a mid-July political rally staged at tiny Henly, near San Marcos.

He went with his father, Sam, Jr., who was now working as a bus inspector for the Texas Railroad Commission. It was a patronage job handed Sam by Pat Neff, a former Texas governor. Neff was now chairman of the railroad commission, a regulatory agency.

The Henly rally was democracy-in-action. Every candidate around was invited. While mothers in bonnets unpacked tin milk pails stuffed with cold chicken legs, the candidates "pressed the flesh," as Lyndon described the practice of shaking hands. Afterwards, the sweltering crowd feasted on watermelon slices and listened to the speeches being made from the back of a wagon.

About mid-afternoon, it came Wally Hopkins' turn. Hopkins was a legislator from Gonzales, Texas. This time around, he was running for the state senate. Ten years older than Lyndon, he walked forward amid the whistling and the "hear-hears" that greeted the announcement of his name.

While Hopkins spoke, Sam Johnson, Jr. began to search for Pat Neff. Neff was locked in a fierce re-election battle with Gregory Hatcher, a former state treasurer. Hatcher wasn't there either, but when his name was called, a man stood and said he had come to speak for the ex-treasurer.

"This man Neff," the fellow was soon saying, "is nothing but a desk-tied, hidebound city slicker. Believe me, he couldn't catch a fish if the directions was written in block-high English on the pole. And he don't hunt. What can a man like that know about runnin' your business and mine? He thinks it can all be learnt out of a book."

The speech was rousingly received. And when no one stepped forward at the call of Pat Neff's name, the Hatcher supporters hooted even louder. In desperation, Sam Johnson tugged on his son's arm. "Get up there, Lyndon, and say something for Pat Neff," he ordered in a loud whisper.

The announcer's introduction was brief. "Sam Johnson's boy, Lyndon," he shouted.

Lyndon leaped onto the wagon and whirled to face the crowd, which was waiting expectantly. "First thing we gotta do," he thundered, "is separate the nonsense from the horse sense. And that won't take but a minute."

The crowd quieted. "Y'all have heard it said that Pat Neff don't hunt or fish." Lyndon paused, his bony hands resting on his high waist. Squinting into the brazen sun, he continued, louder: "I want to remind you of the way those Austin sports come out here into your hills and my hills and shoot our cattle when they're supposed to be huntin' deer. Now, I ask you, do you want a city-slickin' hunter who don't know a cow from a deer to be in charge of your railroad business and your bus lines and your oil business? Or do you want a man whose experience is already tested and proven?"

Speaking without notes, Lyndon held the crowd spellbound for nearly fifteen minutes. In his first genuine on-the-hustings political speech, he was the hit of the Henly rally. Before the last speaker was finished, he had agreed to manage Wally Hopkins' campaign for state senator in the 19th Texas District.

Within a few weeks, with Lyndon's assistance, Hopkins won handsomely. Now it was only a matter of time until politics exercised permanently the option that it had placed on Lyndon Johnson, "Sam Johnson's boy."

Principal William Moyes of Houston's Sam Houston High School thought that he had hired a speech teacher in Lyndon Johnson, but Moyes soon learned that he mostly had hired a debate coach. A debate coach who talked like a football coach. "I'm not interested in how my teams lose," Lyndon stormed at a fellow teacher. "I'm only interested in how they win."

Lyndon served notice on arch-rival San Jacinto High School, which had won the city debate title four years in a row. Lyndon said his teams were going to win the city title, the district title and the *state* title. A startled Principal Moyes soon realized that Lyndon fervently believed in his boast.

Within six weeks, he had transformed debate at Sam Houston High into a holy cause. The school's daily schedule began to hinge on his debate tryouts, which he booked between classes. Each room chose its champions, and these teams then competed for the two school-wide teams, one each for boys and girls. Students not debating were sent to the library to research the 1930-31 debate question: "Resolved, that a substitute for trial by jury should be adopted."

In May at the state capital at Austin, Lyndon's debate teams put their mettle to the full test, having already won at the city and district levels. They were confident, perhaps overly confident, because the girls' team lost in the very first round. And though the two boys, Gene Latimer and Luther Jones, made it to the finals, they lost there on a 3-to-2 vote. The Houston youths wept at the judges' decision. And so did Lyndon.

One day in November, the telephone rang in the school's administrative offices. The man on the other end of the line had just won a special election to the U.S. House of Representatives. He was Richard Kleberg, son of the owner of the famed King Ranch, a cattle barony in South Texas. And he wanted to talk to this Lyndon Johnson whom Wally Hopkins and others had been telling him about.

When he hung up, Lyndon's face was alive with excitement. He turned to a fellow teacher. "Mr. Kleberg wants me to be his private secretary," he blurted. That was how Sam Houston High School lost its new debate coach, and why Lyndon Johnson went to Washington—to fame, to fortune, and eventually to the Presidency of the United States.

Chapter 3

WASHINGTON

Congressman Kleberg and his new secretary caught the train to Washington. Kleberg moved into the fashionable Mayflower Hotel, while Lyndon quickly established himself at the old Dodge Hotel, sharing a room for $20 a month. Usually he took his evening meals at the All States Restaurant, where fifty cents bought all he could eat. Johnson called these economy-styled meals "four-bitters."

Just before payday, Lyndon and the Dodge Hotel crowd often went to Childs Restaurant, where the "house special" was only twenty-five cents, or two bits. The quality of the food didn't worry Lyndon. A greenhorn in the nation's political big league, only one thing mattered to him: discovering where the power in Washington resided, and what keys he needed to open the doors.

"When a group of us went to the House or Senate cafeteria for lunch," recalled Arthur Perry, who was secretary to Senator Tom Connally of Texas, "Lyndon would be at the head of the line." By the time the others arrived at their table, Lyndon would have eaten, says Perry, and was ready to ask questions. "And if he didn't like the answers he got, he would argue. Lyndon was the greatest argufier any of us had ever seen. He wanted to be sure he knew all the answers."

The voters of the 14th Texas District could be thankful that Lyndon was doing his homework. His wealthy employer, "Mister Dick," was often content to lounge around in the overstuffed chairs that outfitted Suite 258 of the Old House Office Building. Kleberg enjoyed the mantle and the manners of a congressman.

Lyndon did get Kleberg to take him on courtesy calls to the two Texas senators, Connally and Morris Sheppard. But the two most valuable friends among congressmen that Lyndon made during his early Capitol Hill days were other Texas members of the House of Representatives, Wright Patman and Sam Rayburn. Both knew Lyndon's father. "Lyndon liked to ask questions about the dirty political fighting that was part of Texas electioneering," remembers Patman, "and he enjoyed hearing whatever you told him about the earlier-day goings in local politics."

In the House of Representatives, Patman and Rayburn were merely two members of a host of powerful Texans. At the very pinnacle of power was Cactus Jack Garner of Uvalde, Texas. On December 7, just eight days after Dick Kleberg officially named Lyndon as his personal secretary, Garner was elected Speaker of the House. That set the stage for an immediate run-in with Kleberg's new secretary.

This dispute, like most Washington disputes, had to do with power. When one man gets more, it is usually at the expense of someone else. In this case, the right to name Texas postmasters, a privilege usually left to each House member in his own district, was challenged by Garner. He quietly passed the word that in the future he would select *all* Texas postmasters. And until Lyndon heard, it looked as if Garner would get away with it.

The news angered the new congressional secretary. He knew that Garner was stealing some of Mister Dick's influence, and he knew that dramatic headlines in the Texas newspapers would harm Garner's plan. So he promptly called on a reporter friend, William S. White, a wire service writer, and gave him the whole story.

Lyndon was right. When the news got back to Texas, the protests were so strong that Garner hastily abandoned his efforts. For days, William White remembered, Garner went around asking other Texas congressmen, with some amusement, "Who is this Lyndon Johnson? Where did Kleberg get a boy with savvy like that?"

Before long, the Old Guard leaders of the Little Congress were wondering the same thing. Suddenly, some upstart named Lyndon Johnson was their speaker. To get the post, he had trampled all over the traditions of this private club for congressional secretaries.

It had started during a nightly bull session at the Dodge Hotel when Lyndon off-handedly asked how the Little Congress chose its officers.

"It's a seniority system, Lyndon," one of the other congressional secretaries replied. "The guy who's been active the longest gets the speaker's chair. It's all done in parliamentary fashion, just like in the big House."

Lyndon nodded. Thoughtfully.

"You going to run for speaker?" the Dodge resident asked.

"I think I will," Lyndon replied.

It was the White Stars again. Only instead of Willard

Deason, Horace Richards, Vernon Whitesides, and Wilton Woods serving as aides, this time it was about a half-dozen of Lyndon's Dodge Hotel buddies.

They divided up the House offices, and each man was assigned to win over several congressional secretaries. Lyndon's campaign pitch was simple: shorter meetings, interesting speakers. Still, the old-timers dawdled. Not until the voting results for new officers was announced did they realize that control of the club had been stolen by Lyndon Johnson.

"Who is that guy?" the defeated candidate shouted. "He comes to one meeting and takes the place over!"

It was, for the record, the same guy who years later would use a similar technique to take over the Democratic leadership of the U.S. Senate.

The first time that Lyndon was ever alone with Claudia Alta Taylor, a shy, brown-eyed girl from Karnack, Texas, was for breakfast in Austin in September, 1934. They had been introduced the previous night by Eugenie Boehringer, a secretary at the state Capitol who knew Lyndon's father. Lyndon already had a date with another girl that evening, but he asked Miss Taylor to meet him for breakfast the next morning. Before the day was over, he proposed marriage to her. "I thought it was some kind of joke," recalls the woman whom the world would someday know by her nickname, Lady Bird.

Lyndon couldn't stay in Texas forever. There was Mister Dick's business to attend back in Washington. And he was planning to enroll in night classes at Georgetown Law School. So Lyndon reluctantly left Lady Bird behind in Texas, promising to write. He called her, too, and mailed her a photograph of himself with this inscription: "For Bird—A lovely girl with ideals, principles, intelligence and refinement, from her sincere admirer, Lyndon."

Seven weeks later, Lyndon was back in Texas, still talking marriage. It occurred on November 17 at St. Mark's Episcopal Church in San Antonio. Dan Quill, the postmaster of San Antonio, was there, and Cecile Harrison, one of Lady Bird's college roommates at the University of Texas. The one missing element was a ring—Lyndon had forgotten one! Quill brought a whole tray to the church, and Lady Bird chose a ring that cost only $2.50. While she didn't know it, Lyndon's new bride had a good reason for being thrifty. Lyndon was about to lose his job.

The reason was Mamie Kleberg, Mister Dick's wife. She could see that Lyndon was running Kleberg's affairs, his office, the man himself—and indeed, she insisted to her jolly-as-you-please husband, Lyndon was getting ready to run for Kleberg's congressional seat.

"Fire him!" she ordered.

Kleberg protested mildly at first, but in the end, during the summer of 1935, he did as his wife demanded. The news stunned Lyndon. Lady Bird was just settling into a routine in their small one-bedroom apartment on Kalorama Road in Washington. There weren't any other jobs readily available. Sam Rayburn had no openings on his Commerce Committee. Another of Lyndon's close congressman friends was Maury Maverick of San Antonio, and Maverick's staff also was full.

One other place that Maverick knew to check was the White House. There, he learned that President Franklin D. Roosevelt, still trying to get the country out of the Great Depression, had just approved the start-up of the National

Youth Administration. Every state needed a NYA director, and Maverick rushed into FDR's office to insist that he had just the man for the Texas job.

Before August was out, Roosevelt called all the state NYA directors back to Washington for a conference, and Lyndon dominated the publicity. It was simple: he just told reporters that he was the nation's youngest NYA director. Also, he came home with more money for his program than most of the NYA state groups because he made a good impression on Aubrey Williams, the national NYA administrator.

Within weeks, Lyndon's Texas NYA operation was a model for the nation. The idea was to keep youngsters in school or, if they were not going to school, to provide them with jobs. Most state NYA groups tried to stay independent of existing agencies, but Lyndon put his NYA youths to work immediately for the Texas highway department, building roadside parks. That worked well, and he quickly offered NYA workers to other agencies. At its height, the Texas NYA had 18,000 boys and girls working part-time while going to school and another 12,000 learning new skills through manual training programs.

One day in early 1936, Eleanor Roosevelt herself bustled through the front door of Lyndon's sixth-floor office in the Littlefield Building in downtown Austin. A flock of women reporters heard the President's wife say that she had come to Texas to see firsthand the splendid job that the Texas NYA director was doing. This kind of flattery merely fueled Lyndon's ego, causing him to put even more pressure on his busy staff.

One day, after about eighteen months, Lyndon went to Houston on NYA business. He stayed overnight with Uncle George Johnson. The next morning, they both saw the

headline about the same time: CONGRESSMAN J. P. BUCHANAN
OF BRENHAM DIES.

"You ought to run," Uncle George told Lyndon. "I think
you'd win, too."

"I think you're right," Lyndon replied.

For a Texas "political daddy"—the kind of adviser that
Sam Rayburn, Wright Patman, and Maury Maverick were in
Washington—Lyndon chose Alvin Wirtz. He was a former
state senator and a powerful corporate attorney with a keen
eye for politics. In the spring of 1937, he had two primary
goals: to get four dams for flood control and power generation
completed with federal money on the Lower Colorado River
and to get Lyndon Johnson into Congress. Wirtz believed that
Johnson could help get him the dams if elected.

Immediately, Wirtz began to deal. He asked Governor
James V. Allred to back Lyndon, but Allred refused. He
learned that Allred planned to announce the date of a special
election to fill Buchanan's seat on March 6, so he urged
Lyndon to make his opening campaign speech on March 5.
Then Wirtz wrote the speech, which Lyndon delivered at San
Marcos.

Lyndon's key point was his backing for Franklin Roosevelt and his New Deal legislation. "If the people of this district
are for bettering the lot of the common man," intoned
Lyndon, "I want to be your congressman. But if the people of
this district don't want to support Roosevelt, then I'll be
content to let some corporation lawyer or lobbyist represent
them."

The election was set for April 10, and the field grew to
nine candidates. Three of the candidates were from Austin,
whose vote was crucial. And four were better known than

Lyndon, which worried Wirtz. What Lyndon needed, he
finally decided, was an issue to isolate himself from the other
eight. He decided to portray Lyndon as the only man among
the eight who was really backing President Roosevelt's plan to
pack the U.S. Supreme Court. The court, opposed to FDR's
New Deal, was declaring the President's acts and actions
unconstitutional, one after the other. So Roosevelt, stung
beyond anger, had decided to press for legislation that would
expand the court from nine to fifteen members, thus giving
him a chance to install a friendly majority.

Most of the candidates in the Texas 10th District's special
election favored the President's court-packing bill, but thanks
to Lyndon's feverish campaigning, this fact was hidden.
Lyndon labeled his opposition "The Eight in the Dark." Even
Roosevelt believed that Johnson was his lone supporter in the
race, and when Postmaster General James A. Farley came to
Texas in March, he put in a good word with reporters for
Roosevelt's "champion." Understandably, the other candidates
protested. But it was too late.

On election night, Lyndon was in an Austin hospital bed,
recovering from an emergency appendectomy. The voting had
been light that day, and Lyndon had received only 27 per cent
of the votes cast. But this was enough. He led from the very
first, carrying Austin with a large vote.

He was now a U.S. congressman. And when FDR came to
Galveston, Texas, in May, 1937, to fish in the Gulf of Mexico,
he asked to see one Texan especially. Lyndon.

Roosevelt had first opposed Lyndon's race for Congress.
His stance came from Aubrey Williams, the NYA administra-
tor. In late February of 1937, Williams had grabbed Thomas
G. "Tommy the Cork" Corcoran, one of FDR's "Brain

Trusters." "For heaven's sake, Tommy," Williams had pled, "call a young man named Lyndon Johnson in Austin and tell him not to run for that House seat. He's a lot more valuable to NYA than he would be in Congress."

Corcoran made the call, but Lyndon had already resigned the NYA post and filed for the congressional race.

By May 11, on the docks of Galveston, he was very much back in Roosevelt's good graces. The President stepped off the Presidential yacht, the U.S.S. *Potomac*, and Lyndon immediately bombarded him with questions about his fishing luck.

"Caught two tarpon," the President replied, grinning. He explained that one of them weighed almost ninety pounds and stretched five feet.

"And how's the family, Mr. President?" Lyndon added.

It is hard to see how the President kept from laughing at this stringbean of an earnest young man from the Texas Hill Country. He was lamp-post-thin from his bout with the diseased appendix, and he was wearing a ridiculous orchid in his lapel. He was dominating the President's time, and he was asking questions that, rightly, were none of his business. Maybe that's why Roosevelt liked him instantly.

Hour after hour, at the President's invitation, Lyndon stayed close by. He rode to the railroad station in Roosevelt's car, and once they were there, FDR invited him to ride along on the Presidential train as far as Fort Worth, 315 miles away. And, Tommy the Cork would later say, "that was all it took—one train ride." En route, Lyndon asked endless questions about the U.S. Navy, remembering that Roosevelt had once served as Assistant Secretary of the Navy. With his youthful eagerness, he won FDR's interest totally.

"Here's a telephone number," FDR told Lyndon as the train approached Fort Worth. "When you get to Washington, call it and ask for Tom. Tell him what we've talked about."

When Lyndon got to Washington, he did three things: he moved into Room 504 of the Old House Office Building, he got himself sworn in as a congressman on May 15, 1937, and he called Tommy the Cork. "You have made yourself a friend in the President," Corcoran told Lyndon. "We'll be in touch."

The next word came from an unexpected source in an unexpected way.

"Young man," a voice called to Lyndon on the House floor one afternoon, "I'm indebted to you for a good dinner and an excellent conversation."

Lyndon stared at Rep. Fred Vinson, a key Democrat. He wasn't sure what Vinson was talking about.

"I was invited to the White House for dinner," Vinson explained with a smile, "and the President was, as always, a most delightful host. I kept wondering just what it was he wanted from me. I knew it was something. Finally he said casually—oh, very casually—'Fred, there's a fine young man just come to the House, and I think he would be a great help on Naval Affairs.' He meant the Naval Affairs Committee, you know."

Lyndon's quick landing of a good committee assignment fueled the widespread belief that he was the President's protégé. The fact that he was invited to a Sunday breakfast at the White House enhanced this image, and other congressmen were soon courting his favor. "His prestige on Capitol Hill was sky-high," said Tommy the Cork. "He could always get to the President."

In 1938 and again in 1940, the image of young Lyndon Johnson as a dashing "can-do" congressman discouraged anyone from running against him in the 10th District of Texas. Each time, he was re-elected without opposition. Because he didn't have to campaign strenuously, he had time to win new friends and promote favorite projects. "He got more projects and more money for his district than any other man in Congress," said Corcoran.

With Lyndon's help, Alvin Wirtz came to Washington in 1939 as Undersecretary of the Interior, and he and Lyndon helped each other. Lyndon worked to get Wirtz' dams finished on the Lower Colorado River, and in turn Wirtz schooled Lyndon in how to solve the problems of bringing electricity to the 10th District's sparsely settled farms.

In July of 1940, Lyndon participated in his first national political convention, going to the Chicago Stadium as vice-chairman of the Texas Democratic delegation. But two other Texans overshadowed his role in getting Roosevelt nominated for an unprecedented third term.

Vice-President Cactus Jack Garner wanted the Presidential nomination, and Sam Rayburn, the Vice-Presidential. Both were disappointed. In fact, Garner's political career was ended by the voting: Roosevelt, 946½; James A. Farley, 72½; John Nance Garner, 61; and Cordell Hull, 6.

The death in September, 1940, of William Bankhead opened to Sam Rayburn a post he had coveted for twenty-five years, that of Speaker of the House. But frankly, he didn't expect to hold the position very long. There was a good chance, he thought, that FDR would be beaten by Wendell Willkie, the Republican candidate. In that case, Lyndon told him that the Republicans might pick up the fifty seats they needed to control the House.

With House Majority Leader John McCormack of Massachusetts, Rayburn hurried to the White House to tell Roosevelt that the Democratic National Congressional Committee had hard work to do. And, Rayburn said, he didn't think the committee chairman, Patrick Drewry of Virginia, could do the job.

"Who do you think can?" asked Roosevelt.

"Let's put Lyndon Johnson in charge and give him a free hand," Rayburn suggested.

It was done, and when the Republicans not only failed to gain fifty seats but in fact lost five more on election night—November 5, 1940—Lyndon deserved some, and took most, of the credit. With this new national status, he began to think about running for the U.S. Senate. There were just two problems. Tom Connally and Morris Sheppard. Both were unbeatable.

But then, on April 9, 1941, Morris Sheppard died of a brain hemorrhage. . . .

Chapter 4

A CRAZY RACE

The voices in Lyndon's head had only one message: run.
These were the voices of Sam Ealy Johnson, Sr., Sam, Jr.,
Rebekah Johnson, Professor Greene, and Uncle George, all
echoing together: *My grandson, a U.S. senator. . . . A man can
serve his country in the United States Senate. . . . I think you
can win, Lyndon. . . . the United States Senate.* Even before
the short, happy, much-admired Morris Sheppard had suc-
cumbed to his fatal attack, Lyndon had decided that, yes, he
would make the race to fill the first Texas vacancy in the U.S.
Senate in thirteen years.

He had no idea of what was coming, of the free-for-all
ahead. He didn't suspect that he faced one of the weirdest
campaigns in American political history. That was because
Lyndon didn't know that Governor Wilbert Lee O'Daniel also
planned to run. And "Pappy Lee" O'Daniel, a Texas flour mill
owner, was a clown.

O'Daniel campaigned with a hillbilly band, The Light
Crust Doughboys, and he sang songs for the voters like "Your
Own Sweet Darling Wife" and "The Boy Who Never Gets

Too Big to Comb His Mother's Hair." Such antics, understandably, embarrassed many Texas voters. But, on the other hand, they attracted a lot of voters, too.

It was O'Daniel's right and duty to set a date for a special election to fill Sheppard's seat, and he finally announced the election for Saturday, June 28.

The law also instructed the governor to appoint an interim senator until the election. For a few days, O'Daniel considered the appointment for himself. Then he decided to appoint a weak interim senator, someone who couldn't possibly win in the special June election.

The appointee was Andrew Jackson Houston, the sick, enfeebled eighty-six-year-old son of General Sam Houston, the early-day Texas hero. Many Texans were aghast, and their concern was soon justified. The aging Houston traveled to Washington, attended two Senate meetings and then was hospitalized. He died on June 26, two days before the special election back home.

Unfortunately, the circus had only begun. With Ringmaster O'Daniel's whistle, the candidates poured into the Big Top.

There were twenty-nine in all, and each had his peculiarities. There was a bootlegger, an admitted kidnapper, and a chiropractor. There was a Baptist preacher who was running on a platform of prohibition and a Naval Academy graduate who wanted to declare immediate war with Japan. Another candidate, a geologist, insisted that, if elected, he would award $5 pensions to everyone, and Congressman Martin Dies, Sr. said the country needed to rid itself of Communists. Two candidates claimed links to famous early-day Texans. Two wore full beards, and one candidate, laxative manufacturer Hal Collins, gave away free mattresses at his rallies.

Another candidate was Dr. John R. Brinkley of Del Rio, who owned one of the world's most powerful radio stations. When not campaigning, he sold elixirs made of dried goat glands. The attorney general of Texas, young Gerald Mann, was running. So were two Republicans named Politte Elvins and Enoch Fletcher, and a Communist named Homer Brooks. Cactus Jack Garner and a former governor, James E. "Pa" Ferguson, had thought about running but decided against it.

Rep. Wright Patman also wanted to run, but the word came from the White House: Don't. A savvy politician, Patman realized that Roosevelt favored Lyndon's candidacy, which he was about to announce.

Lyndon came to Texas on San Jacinto Day and addressed the legislature about mobilizing for war. It was a smooth, stirring speech, prepared by White House speech writers. While in Austin, Lyndon also put the question to Governor O'Daniel: Are you going to run? The governor said no, lying.

Lyndon rushed back to Washington, happy at what O'Daniel had told him. At FDR's urging, he announced his candidacy from the steps of the White House, and reporters rushed to Roosevelt, asking if he was endorsing Lyndon. The President's answer was a political classic for what it did and did not say.

"First, it is up to the people of Texas to elect the man they want as their senator," President Roosevelt said, unsmilingly. "Second, everybody knows that I cannot enter a primary election. And third"—his eyes began to twinkle—"to be truthful all I can say is that Lyndon Johnson is a very old, old friend of mine. And you can quote me directly."

So Lyndon was in the race, and he was going to get the full support of the national Democratic leadership. That was good, and bad. It might help him to win in Texas, but if he lost, it would greatly weaken his influence in Washington.

On May 4, the respected Belden Opinion Poll of Texas announced that Governor O'Daniel was the leading candidate, with 32.8 per cent of the voters. Attorney General Mann had 28.2 per cent; Martin Dies, 27.9; and Lyndon, only 9.3.

O'Daniel hadn't even announced his candidacy—and he didn't until May 19. But Alvin Wirtz hadn't resigned as Undersecretary of the Interior to direct the campaign of a man who was going to get only 9.3 per cent of the vote. Lyndon had kicked his campaign off at San Marcos on May 3, the day before the Belden Poll was released. After that, Wirtz said that they would flood Texas with the Johnson-for-Senator message.

They decided on "Roosevelt and Unity" as their campaign banner. At every campaign stop, Lyndon spoke while standing in front of a huge blown-up photograph that showed him shaking hands with the President.

Then came the spring Texas rains, and the candidates cancelled their speeches. All except Lyndon. He kept on, wading through rain-filled gutters and wearing damp clothes. After a few days, he ended up in a hospital with a severe throat infection. After ten days in bed, he figured that his chances of winning were finished. Period.

The true picture came into focus with the next Belden Poll. Governor O'Daniel had dropped from 32.8 to 22.4 per cent. Gerald Mann slipped from 28.2 to 26.8 per cent. Martin Dies went from 27.9 to 26.2 per cent. And Lyndon? He had gained, shooting from 9.3 to 17.6 per cent.

It was no mystery, at least to Alvin Wirtz. While Lyndon was hospitalized, Wirtz and two friends had stepped into his speaking engagements and his radio programs. While the other candidates ducked out of the rain, Lyndon's friends had kept hammering at the issues, keeping Lyndon's name in the headlines.

Headlines were something that Washington could help with, and Roosevelt assigned his assistant press secretary to write telegrams of support for dispatch to Lyndon at key moments. The President's press secretary was told to drum up interest in Lyndon among the Washington reporters who were read back in Texas. In addition, Harold Young, a top Vice-Presidential aide, was ordered to Texas as a campaign assistant to Alvin Wirtz.

It was impossible for the other candidates to ignore Roosevelt's intense interest in Lyndon's chances, and they tried to turn this to their advantage. Attorney General Mann, who was waging a humorless campaign, hinted that Lyndon was a blind supporter of Roosevelt's, a "yes-man" without peer.

"Yes," Lyndon replied, "I am a yes-man for the President. I am a yes-man for everything that is American. I am a yes-man for anything that will aid in the defense of this Republic. I am a yes-man to the Commander-in-Chief, as every good soldier should be in time of emergency. But you are not electing a yes-man. You are electing a man to whom Roosevelt will say *yes*."

For voters repelled by Governor O'Daniel's empty campaign talk, Lyndon offered a platform built on his "Roosevelt and Unity" idea. He called for aiding England with war materials and developing a two-million-man army. He wanted to draft executives to run defense plants and unemployed women to make arms. And then he called for U.S. military forces to occupy Greenland, Iceland, Dakar, the Canary Islands, and Cape Verde.

With the election drawing nearer and nearer, some of the

twenty-nine candidates dropped out. Dr. Brinkley, the goat-gland man, quit on June 6. Rep. Martin Dies began to fall behind. Finally, Governor O'Daniel quit feuding with the Texas Legislature and hit the campaign trail. And that was when the circus began its grand finale. Only the star wasn't O'Daniel. It was Lyndon.

Lyndon slapped at a mosquito, flattening him dead. The muggy Texas air was holding to its reputation. The speech in his hands felt clammy and limp, like a drooping flower. Even with his coat off, the back of his shirt was soggy with perspiration.

He guessed that the Johnson Swingsters were probably soaked. Every little while, Lyndon caught a glimpse of their white dinner jackets, bobbing on the bandstand in one corner of the town's courthouse square. They were playing jazz for the townspeople—with their coats on.

Lyndon had to hand it to Alvin Wirtz. The idea of a traveling patriotic rally—a rally for "Roosevelt and Unity"—was working splendidly. A *smash* hit, you might say. Look at that crowd over there. Probably wasn't a hundred persons in the whole town who hadn't come.

Lyndon listened to Sophia Parker. When she warbled "I Am an American," she put everything she had into it, and it was a sight to see. Two hundred and eighty-five pounds dressed in a spreading white evening gown decorated with red, white and blue trimmings. They called her the "Kate Smith of the South."

Sophia was doing it again. This time, the audience was singing along, and a dog, too. The idea of Alvin Wirtz had been to out-do Pappy Lee O'Daniel when it came to entertaining the good voter folks. So, like the weather, the show had something for everybody. There was the jazz of the Johnson Swingsters, a minstrel act, dancing girls, singers, a comedy act, a drawing for free savings bonds, and—of course—the all-important patriotic pageant.

". . . and now," Lyndon heard his radio-trained announcer call out, "here it is, 'The Spirit of American Unity,' paid for by friends of the President!"

The first part of the script was mournful. It could be a funeral scene, judging from the music the Swingsters were playing. "There was hunger," the announcer read slowly. "There was sadness, and there was despair loose in this land. And then . . ."

Lyndon smiled. The man on the cornet was getting good at blowing that bugle charge. *Sounds like Teddy Roosevelt attacking San Juan Hill,* he thought.

"And then," the announcer shouted again, "in 1932 . . . along came a man named *Roosevelt!*" The crowd cheered, and several dogs howled. "He saved the banks! He put the people to work. He gave us the CCC and the NYA, the NRA and the REA." The Swingsters were playing bouncy music now, with a happy beat. "People," said the announcer, his deep voice reading smoothly, "were eating chicken and ice cream again!"

Lyndon couldn't see that far, but he knew that the moderator's face was taking on another frown. "But all this could be swept away," the announcer said. The Swingsters were playing funeral music again. "So the people re-elected our great President!" Swinging music. Then silence. Even Lyndon's heart beat a little faster as he waited.

The announcer said, "Hitler came and Germany threatened the world again. What could Americans do about it?

They elected Franklin Delano Roosevelt to a third term!" The band played happy music, the crowd cheered, and Lyndon again checked the pages of his speech.

The band was playing "God Bless America" very softly and rather slowly. "Franklin Roosevelt needed a man who loved his country, who loved the people," the announcer was saying. "President Roosevelt endorsed this man. This man is *Lyndon Johnson. . . .*"

Lyndon hurried toward the crowd from the rear, straightening his hat and his coat as he went. Up ahead, he could see the dignitaries standing on the stage. The singing, the comedy, the pageant—it was over, and the time had come to explain why Lyndon Johnson would make a better United States senator from Texas than Wilbert Lee O'Daniel, Gerald Mann, Martin Dies, Politte Elvins, Enoch Fletcher, Homer Brooks, and the others.

Already, the crowd had been there more than an hour, but Lyndon noted with satisfaction that nobody was leaving.

The morning after the June 28 election, the headlines of the Houston *Post* read: JOHNSON, WITH 5,152 VOTE LEAD, APPEARS ELECTED. O'Daniel was second, with 162,124 votes. Gerald Mann's 134,871 and Dies' 71,275 trailed. But Governor O'Daniel wasn't conceding, and Alvin Wirtz had a good idea why. The whiskey lobby was at work.

O'Daniel was against liquor, and the liquor lobbyists wanted him out of Texas. The best way to get him out was to send him to Washington as U.S. senator. So, slowly, vote totals began to change. They changed in the rural East Texas counties, and they changed in the heavily Mexican-American counties in South Texas. And suddenly, instead of a 5,152 vote lead, Lyndon trailed by 1,311 votes out of nearly 600,000.

It was strange. Many Texans believed it was highway

robbery. But Lyndon insisted, "No, no, that is this ball game. My vacation is over and we'll play again some other time." One of the reasons that he didn't want a full-scale investigation was that he had spent far more money on his campaign than the law allowed, some reports said more than $500,000.

One of the first changes he noticed when he returned to Washington was that he was no longer the fair-haired boy of the White House. "Next time," snapped the President, "sit on the ballot boxes!"

Chapter 5

A TIME TO CHANGE

Off to the side of the plane, an airman offered a hasty salute, and the pilot, Lt. Walter Greer, shoved the throttles forward. The *Heckling Hare* shuddered, lunged and hummed fiercely before it flew.

From a perch just behind the cockpit of the B-26, Lyndon watched the runway disappear. In its place, the curl-tipped waters of the South Pacific lapped lazily at the shores of Australia.

As Lt. Greer steered the plane on out to sea, Lyndon thought it was all so improbable. The ocean was so beautiful, so peaceful. And yet the *Heckling Hare* was loaded with bombs. On this 9th of June, 1942, they were outbound from Port Moresby, New Guinea, to the island of Lae, on a mission of war. The Japanese had struck murderously at Pearl Harbor on December 7, and Lyndon had voted for war on December 8. The next day, since he was a reserve lieutenant commander, the Navy had ordered him to duty.

Watching Lt. Greer and his co-pilot as they eyed the skies for enemy planes, Lyndon mused how the Navy assignment to

San Francisco had almost been a terrible trap. A desk job was not exactly his idea of wartime service. The personal appeal to President Roosevelt had been risky, busy as the Commander-in-Chief was with Prime Minister Churchill's visit and other war duties. But it had worked. The hard-pressed Roosevelt had suggested that he leave on a fact-finding mission to the Pacific Theater.

And facts. . . . What was *that*? Lyndon heard it again, and in the cockpit below, he could see Lt. Greer and the co-pilot frowning at the portside engine. The engine coughed again. Lyndon sensed that the plane was slowing, and that would make it easy prey, he knew, for any of the enemy's swift Zero fighters.

Suddenly, one of the *Heckling Hare*'s gunners shouted, "Zeroes!"

Ping! *Ping-ping*. High-caliber bullets began bouncing off and through the *Heckling Hare* so rapidly that Lyndon lost count. He was about to duck when Lt. Greer put the *Heckling Hare* in a steep dive. The craft bucked as Greer jettisoned the bombs and headed furiously for a nearby cloud.

The cloud at least sheltered them from the enemy's view. After checking to see that no one was hurt, Greer called out, "We're going on down to the deck." With that warning, he put the plane into another dive, and they were soon skimming the waves. Fifty, twenty, sometimes ten feet off.

Suddenly, Lyndon was thinking about a speech he had made last August to the House of Representatives about continuing the U.S. draft. "I know how Texas boys feel," he had bragged. "I am one of them. Texas boys come from a race of men who fought for their freedom at the Alamo and Goliad and San Jacinto. . . . Texas boys prefer service now to slavery later."

Now, this Texas boy was skimming the Pacific Ocean at 210 miles an hour, trying desperately to elude eight enemy fighter planes. Ducking his head so he could look out of the B-26's squarish windows, he could see nothing but the blurred blue ocean. Lyndon felt like a rodeo rider on a bronc charging out of a chute. Only there wasn't any soft dirt to be bucked off into—just a big wide, wet sea.

But one by one, the pursuing Japanese fighter planes gave up and flew home. They couldn't get through the fire from the B-26's seven fifty-caliber machine guns. The *Heckling Hare* and its shaken occupants limped back to Port Moresby, where everyone told his story. And Lyndon's quickly reached the ears of Lt. Col. Douglas MacArthur, the Southwest Pacific commander. When Lyndon announced plans to leave Australia on June 18, MacArthur swiftly acted on a plan to gain Lyndon's goodwill. He knew that Lyndon claimed to be a close friend of President Roosevelt's, and he desperately wanted Roosevelt to realize the importance of the Southwest Pacific war.

That very day, in ceremonies in MacArthur's office, Lyndon received the Silver Star for "gallantry in action." Even halfway around the world, Lyndon couldn't get away from politics. For no one else on the *Heckling Hare* was honored, not even Lt. Greer, the iron-nerved pilot.

The Lyndon Johnson who returned to Washington in July, 1942, was not the same Lyndon Johnson who had departed six months earlier. One change was in his physical appearance. In the Fiji Islands, he had become ill and was rushed to a hospital. While fighting pneumonia, his gangling frame lost thirty pounds.

But more than that had changed. Politically, the Johnson star had lost a lot of its glitter. The reasons were many and complex. If anything, Lyndon was largely a victim of circumstances. Early in his congressional career, Lyndon's personality and his political style had fit neatly into Franklin Roosevelt's New Deal. The password of the New Deal had been "momentum"—move, move, move. Let's get the country *moving* again! And just about everyone in Washington agreed that, if anything, Congressman Lyndon Johnson was a *mover*.

Then came his defeat by Governor O'Daniel in the '41 Senate race and suddenly Lyndon wasn't moving nearly so fast. And not long after that came a world war, and the country didn't need all the economic hoopla and the razzmatazz of FDR's New Deal. From the politician-in-charge, Roosevelt became more the commander-in-chief. And as his priorities changed, so did the value to him of politicians like Lyndon.

It took Lyndon time to realize this. The minute he returned to Washington, he had demanded an audience with the President, and he told a mournful story: military equipment was short in the Southwest Pacific area, many officers were unqualified, and Japan's deft Zero fighter planes were mopping up the skies.

Hungry for headlines, Lyndon began to watch the activities of a senator from Missouri, Harry Truman. On orders from the Senate, Truman was regularly investigating the nation's defense industries, looking for signs of graft, waste, and excess profits. What was good for the Senate, Lyndon decided, would be just as good for the House. Rep. Carl Vinson agreed to name Lyndon as chairman of a five-man investigative subcommittee to the Naval Affairs Committee, which Vinson headed. Within days, Lyndon was busy looking for things to criticize in the Navy's procurement program.

The subcommittee was largely a one-man affair. "The

other members were relatively contented men," said a sub-committee employee. "They weren't a bundle of nerves like Johnson. They weren't going to kill themselves working—and he knew it."

His 10th District congressional seat was safe for another two years. Without his knowledge, Alvin Wirtz and Tom Miller, the mayor of Austin, had managed a write-in campaign in his behalf that spring while he was in the South Pacific. Once they had gotten his name on the ballot, re-election had been automatic, since no one else ran.

More and more, Lyndon began to think about wealth and how little he had of it. One of his ambitions was to become a millionaire. And yet for the first six months of 1942, at his insistence, he had been paid the paltry salary of a Navy lieutenant commander, just $250 a month. That was nearly $600 a month less than he had been paid as a congressman.

That fall, Alvin Wirtz finally hit on a plan to make Lyndon rich. It involved, improbably, a radio station, KTBC of Austin, Texas.

So involved was Wirtz' scheme to get ownership of the station for Lyndon and Lady Bird that it resembled a chess game. Two other parties held options to buy the station, and Wirtz had to frighten them off. Then he had to buy the station, get the Federal Communications Commission to approve the sale and get the station's wattage increased.

The FCC approved the sale on January 25, 1943. Lady Bird was listed as the owner so Lyndon would be shielded from "conflict of interest" charges. Later, in the first of many FCC favors to the Johnsons, Station KTBC received its own wavelength and an increase in power to 1000 watts. Within five years, Lyndon was telling people that—at last—he was a millionaire.

On March 19, 1944, he also became a father. The first person he telephoned with the news was Sam Rayburn. "It's a red, crying, screaming baby girl!" he shouted to Rayburn.

The next day they named her Lynda Bird after her father and her mother.

"Mister Chairman," Alvin Wirtz was shouting. "Mister Chairman!"

Above the angry roar of the crowd, Lyndon could hear a gavel pounding madly in the Senate chambers at the Texas Capitol Building, and he frowned deeply. A cagey George Butler, the state Democratic chairman, had just outsmarted an equally cagey Alvin Wirtz, and Lyndon now realized that Wirtz was facing defeat.

Wirtz had come to the 1944 state Democratic convention as the leader of the Texas loyalists, those party members still backing President Roosevelt. Butler was the spokesman for the Texas regulars, who were anti-Roosevelt. And the regulars, with Butler as chairman, were in control of the convention.

To dislodge the regulars, Wirtz had planned to act while many of the delegates were out of the meeting hall. If he moved immediately following the keynote speech, he believed that he could nominate former Governor Jimmy Allred as temporary chairman and get him elected before most of the absent delegates returned.

But, Lyndon realized, Butler had just thwarted Wirtz' plan. Butler had proposed that the keynote speech be dropped, and he had just nominated former Governor Dan Moody, a regular, for temporary chairman. Wirtz had argued hard for the keynote address. Seeing that he was defeated, he had then nominated Allred against Moody. And there was the vote on the blackboard: Moody 940 7/12, Allred 774 5/12.

Alvin wasn't giving up. "I move that we order the Texas Presidential electors to cast their votes for the Presidential nominee who wins the popular vote in the November general election," he said swiftly. There, now all of Wirtz' cards were on the table. This was what he was really after. He was afraid that the Texas regulars would order the state's representatives to the national Electoral College to vote against Roosevelt, even if he won the '44 election in Texas.

And that's exactly what the regulars intended to do.

No sooner was Wirtz finished with his motion than the convention dissolved in noisy disorder. To his right, up near the speaker's stand, Lyndon could see a fistfight. He recognized the men. Both were former state senators, one a loyalist and the other a regular. From one corner of the hall to the other, the delegates had become a mob.

It's about time for a compromise, Lyndon thought to himself when the shouting continued. He walked onto the platform, heading toward Chairman Butler. To his surprise and dismay, his appearance caused the crowd to grow even angrier.

"Let's get that Roosevelt pin-up boy out of here," a delegate jeered.

"Throw that turncoat yes-man off the platform," another yelled.

"No deals with the New Dealer," screamed a third.

Lyndon felt the blood rush to his face. He quickly saw that there wasn't much room for compromise. He returned to the floor and watched Butler, pounding that gavel as if he were driving a rivet, bring an end to the commotion. Quickly, the convention tossed Wirtz' motion out, 952 to 695. The regulars were in total control.

Out of the corner of his eye, Lyndon spotted Mrs. Alfred

Taylor, a loyalist leader, hurrying toward the microphone. He knew without being told what she was about to do. And she did. "I would like to invite all the loyal friends of our dear President to join with me and Mr. Wirtz in a separate convention in the chambers of the Texas House," she said firmly.

The exodus was on. Though he didn't approve, Lyndon followed the river of loyalist delegates hurrying toward the doors. As they left, the regulars' organist was playing "Good Night, Ladies."

That year, Lyndon didn't attend the national Democratic convention. If the events at the state convention hadn't been insult enough, the Texas regulars had provided an opponent for him in the '44 primary. His name was Buck Taylor, and his campaign approach was to try to smear Lyndon as a "nigger-lover." Taylor claimed Lyndon planned to destroy the white Texas citizens' hold on the election process.

Lyndon knew that Taylor was referring to a U.S. Supreme Court decision issued in April, 1944. It struck down any racial bars that prevented Texas Negroes from voting in the state primary elections. Taylor's reasoning was this: The Supreme Court was Roosevelt's court, and Lyndon was Roosevelt's friend. Therefore, Lyndon deserved credit for permitting Negroes to vote in the Texas Democratic primaries.

The only satisfaction that Lyndon got out of the '44 congressional primary was that he swamped Buck Taylor by a margin of 2½ to 1.

Franklin Roosevelt died on April 12, 1945, and Lyndon got the news on Capitol Hill about 5 P.M. from Sam Rayburn and others who had been visiting in Rayburn's private lounge, the "Board of Education," where friends met to talk and drink together. One of those present was William S. White, *The New York Times'* reporter. He asked Lyndon for his reaction to the President's death, and his reply was carried in the next morning's *Times*.

"They called the President a dictator and some of us they called yes-men," Lyndon recalled. "Sure, I yessed him plenty of times—because I thought he was right—and I'm not sorry for a single *yes* I ever gave. I have seen the President in all kinds of moods—at breakfast, at lunch, at dinner—and never once in my five terms did he ever ask me to vote a certain way, or even suggest it. And when I voted against him—as I have plenty of times—he never said a word."

Already, even before Roosevelt's body was in the grave, Lyndon was beginning to declare his independence of the New Deal and the FDR image. The shouts hurled at him at the state Democratic convention were still ringing in his ears. The New Deal, he could see, was dead. The back of the Depression had been broken. It was a time, Lyndon judged, to take a more conservative stance, especially if he was going to win any statewide races back home.

But it was by no means certain, Lyndon soon realized, that he was going to be re-elected to his congressional seat in '46. Again, he had an opponent, a district judge named Hardy Hollers. Hollers was full of questions about Lyndon's financial affairs. And it was his opinion, free for the asking, that Lyndon was an out-and-out thief. "If the U.S. Attorney was on the job," Hollers contended, "Lyndon Johnson would be in the federal penitentiary instead of in the Congress of the United States."

Lyndon focused on the abundance of "pork-barrel" projects that his efforts in Washington had brought to the 10th District. But, plainly, he was running scared and campaigning fiercely—for the first time, really, since 1937. He didn't quit campaigning until Election Day, and he was greatly relieved when the vote totals came in. He won handily.

Before the year was out, Lady Bird was pregnant again, and in July, 1947, a second daughter was born to the Johnsons. They named her Lucy Baines, and Lyndon joked that now everyone in the family could use the same luggage, since all had the initials LBJ.

Later, Lyndon was no longer in the mood for jokes. If he was going to be a U.S. senator at the age of forty, he had to run in the '48 Democratic primary. The good news was that Senator W. Lee O'Daniel was completely out of favor with the voters. The bad news was that the Belden Poll for March, 1948, showed Coke Stevenson leading Lyndon by a three-to-one margin in a race for the U.S. Senate.

Chapter 6

ROUTE TO THE SENATE

The helicopter swept toward a clearing, usually a baseball field or a pasture at the edge of town. With a deafening roar, the *Johnson City Windmill* settled to the ground in a swirl of dust and out the door stepped Lyndon Johnson. He was campaigning again for the U.S. Senate.

Sometimes, Lyndon didn't land. He just hovered close to a farmhouse or over the main street of a country town and talked to the people through a loudspeaker on the blunt-nosed copter. "Hello, down there," he would shout. "This is your friend Lyndon Johnson of Johnson City, your candidate for the Senate, dropping by to say good morning."

The helicopter was scorned by some of Lyndon's opponents in the 1948 primary race.

Ex-Governor Coke Stevenson—the taciturn rancher with the nickname "Calculating Coke"—dismissed suggestions that he get a helicopter. "No, thanks, I'll keep my campaign down to earth," he joked. The third candidate, George Peddy, a Houston attorney, suggested that "the *Johnson City Windmill* is the name of both the helicopter and its occupant."

For Alvin Wirtz, who was again managing Lyndon's campaign, the whole affair seemed like a replay of the campaign of '41. Just as before, they had hardly started campaigning when Lyndon went to the hospital, this time with a painful kidney stone. After treatment at the Mayo Clinic in Minnesota, Lyndon returned home to learn that his main opponents were barely campaigning. As a result, he was gaining. The Belden Poll for June 20 gave Stevenson 46.6 per cent, Johnson 36.8 and Peddy 12.

Again, Wirtz decided, Lyndon needed a gimmick. Not a traveling patriotic spectacular, since this time they weren't fighting W. Lee O'Daniel. But something that traveled faster than the old Plymouth car that Coke Stevenson was riding in from town to town. That's when Wirtz decided on the helicopter.

Instead of "Roosevelt and Unity," Lyndon's slogan this time around was "Peace, Preparedness, Progress." By "peace," he really meant mobilizing for war ("We went into two world wars unprepared and let's not do it again"). By "preparedness," he meant massive rearmament ("I stopped the sale at junkyard prices of our war plants, worth $1,258,000,000"). By "progress," he meant keeping President Truman from meddling in the states' affairs ("I believe in a federal policy that leaves to the states those matters which are state functions, like civil rights").

The main difference between the special Senate election of '41 and the Democratic primary election of '48, Wirtz soon learned, was in the outcome. It wasn't even close. The results reported by the Texas Election Bureau late on election day—July 24, 1948—showed Stevenson with 477,077 votes to 405,617 for Lyndon. Now there had to be a runoff, and if Lyndon lost, his political career was probably over.

"In New York," Tommy the Cork Corcoran, the Roosevelt Brain Truster, once said, "people make money. In Texas, they make politics."

Corcoran was right. Since the Civil War, Texas has served as a kind of academy for national politicians. Or, more accurately, a kind of commando training camp for politicians. Texas politics has always been tough, even brutal.

The most brutal election of all was one of the earliest. In 1873, E. Jack Davis, a carpetbagging Republican, sought re-election as governor. No Texas governor was ever hated more. He had set up the nation's first state police, raised taxes, and sold the voters out to banking and industrial interests. The result was a bloody election in 1873. Election officials were murdered, voters were threatened, and ballot boxes stolen.

The Democrats won overwhelmingly, but that didn't oust Davis. He ordered the state's Supreme Court to throw the election results out. The hated ex-governor surrendered his office only after an armed mob of Democrats marched on the Capitol on January 19, 1874.

The election of 1873 seemed to set a pattern for Texas politics. In one of the 1890-era elections, a candidate used murder and fraud as routine campaign tactics. Later, the Texas branch of the Ku Klux Klan practiced their violent brand of Texas politics. One night Lyndon's father, Sam Ealy, Jr., and two of his brothers stayed up all night armed with shotguns, waiting. The Klan had threatened to kill Sam because of his strong legislative speeches against racism. ("I was only a fifteen-year-old boy in the middle of all this," Lyndon later noted, "and I was fearful that my daddy would be taken out and tarred and feathered.")

By Lyndon Johnson's time, election-day murders were rare. But election-day fraud in Texas was as common as live oak trees in Blanco County. Any sharp political strategist knew this, including President Roosevelt. That was why, after Lyndon lost to Governor O'Daniel in 1941, Roosevelt had warned Lyndon to sit on the ballot boxes next time. And that's what Lyndon intended to do.

"I basically lost the election in 1941, I think," said John Connally, the young South Texan that Lyndon had brought to Washington in 1939 as his secretary. "I told some of the election officials in South Texas to go ahead and report their complete returns to the Texas Election Bureau. That way, the other side knew exactly how many votes they needed."

This time, expecting the '48 runoff election to be razor-close, Lyndon's advisers were prepared to play the guessing game themselves.

The voting was close. At midnight of election day, August 28, Coke Stevenson led Lyndon by 470,681 to 468,787. By mid-afternoon on Sunday, that lead had dropped to 315 votes. By Sunday night, Lyndon led by 693 votes. By Monday night, Stevenson was in front by 119 votes. Then, on Thursday, the Texas Election Bureau announced that it was all over: Stevenson had won by 362 votes.

But the election bureau was premature. The next day its spokesman announced that Stevenson's lead was only 114 votes.

John Connally knew exactly what was happening. "At one time," he later explained, "we had twenty-five or thirty counties—maybe even fifty—where we were leading, holding back reports on their complete returns. If we weren't leading, we let them go ahead and report them promptly. So our figures were better than the election bureau's because we knew everything it knew plus a lot it didn't."

Even now, the vote total wasn't complete. To their

horror, the Stevenson supporters learned that Alvin Wirtz and John Connally had suddenly left Austin. At least one of them was headed south to George Parr country.

Parr was a political dictator. They called him "the Duke of Duval" because he ruled Duval County, Texas, with an iron fist. He also ruled Jim Wells and Nueces counties. The residents of the three counties were mostly Mexican-Americans, laboring people who were poorly educated. Political boss Parr gave them jobs, paid their poll taxes for them, and voted the entire counties as he pleased. It wasn't unusual for Duval County to report hundreds of votes for the candidate or cause that Parr favored, and no votes for the opposition.

For years, Coke Stevenson had enjoyed Parr's support. In his 1944 race for governor, for example, Stevenson had received 3,310 Duval County votes to a combined 17 votes for his opponents.

But on September 4, Stevenson learned that he had lost Parr's backing. After talking with John Connally, Parr suddenly announced an error of 203 votes in Box 13 in Jim Wells County, 202 of these for Lyndon. By adding these 202 votes, the election bureau now said that Lyndon had the Democratic Senate primary by 87 votes. Stevenson was furious. "I was beaten by a stuffed ballot box," he insisted. "And I can prove it!"

But Stevenson knew he couldn't get anywhere by arguing. He needed evidence.

He hired two ex-FBI agents and sent them to George Parr country. When Parr laughed the Stevenson representatives out of his office, Stevenson persuaded Capt. Frank Hamer, a famous Texas Ranger, to help them get to the suspect Box 13 voters' list. It was locked in an Alice, Texas, bank vault. On the morning of September 9, Hamer and the ex-FBI men were able to examine the list for a few minutes.

A strange list, they decided. The last 203 names on the list all appeared in the same ink, the same handwriting and were listed in *alphabetical* order. The odds that 203 voters would have walked in and registered in perfect alphabetical order were indeed small.

The official at the Parr-owned bank wouldn't let the trio of inspectors copy the list, but they quickly memorized five names. Later, after they checked, the Stevenson men reported that three of the persons named were dead and the other two swore that they hadn't voted in the election.

Mere evidence of fraud wasn't enough either, Stevenson realized. He had to find someone in authority to throw the Box 13 results out.

The first authority to appeal to was the Democratic Executive Committee of Jim Wells County. But when, on September 10, the Stevenson forces tried to present their case to the Executive Committee, the Johnson forces got a court injunction ordering the committee not to rule on the Box 13 vote.

Next came the state Democratic Executive Committee, and on the night of September 13, in Fort Worth, Texas, the group listened to arguments from both sides. Earlier that afternoon, a subcommittee had ruled 4-to-3 in favor of Stevenson. And late that night, vote of the whole committee ended in a 28-to-28 deadlock.

Committee chairman Robert W. Calvert said he wasn't going to break the tie. The issue would have to be debated the next day at the state Democratic convention. About that time, a man was heard to shout from the doorway, "Let me through, let me through!" He charged into the meeting room and announced, "I'm Charley Gibson from Amarillo and I vote for Lyndon."

So Stevenson lost 29-to-28. When he also lost at the state convention the next day, he decided to appeal to the federal courts. "About a half-million Texans voted for me and they have been defrauded and robbed," he asserted.

Before daylight on September 15, two Stevenson aides roused Federal District Court Judge T. Whitfield Davidson out of bed at his East Texas farm. When they left, they had a temporary court order keeping Lyndon's name off the ballot. Also, the judge had set a hearing in Fort Worth on September 21.

The Johnson forces were stunned. The deadline for getting on the November election ballot was September 17.

Wirtz and two other Johnson lawyers appealed to the Texas Supreme Court, but got nowhere. And at Judge Davidson's hearing on the 21st, the result was the same. The judge bluntly told the Johnson lawyers, "There has not been one word of evidence to disprove this plaintiff's claim that he has been robbed of a seat in the United States Senate." The next day, Davidson named a special United States commissioner to investigate the Stevenson charges and dismissed the hearing until September 27.

The commissioner, William Robert Smith, found that most of the witnesses he needed were missing and most of the evidence destroyed. But it didn't matter. For when Lyndon's lawyers tried and failed to get the U.S. Fifth Circuit Court of Appeals to dismiss Judge Davidson's order, they moved to Washington. And there, they got the results they were after.

On September 28, Justice Hugo Black of the United States Supreme Court was persuaded to sign an order canceling Judge Davidson's ruling. Now Lyndon's name could go on the ballot. The reason Justice Black gave for issuing the order was that federal courts had no jurisdiction over state elections. But it was no secret that he was a close, warm friend of the chief lawyer for the Johnson cause, attorney Abe Fortas of Washington.

A few weeks later, in the November general election, Lyndon beat Jack Porter, the Republican candidate, by 702,985 votes to 349,665.

Just as grandfather Sam Ealy Johnson, Sr. had predicted, Lyndon was a member of the United States Senate at the age of forty. But it had been a vicious, costly race, and Lyndon was in no mood to be charitable. He denounced Stevenson as a poor loser, and he headed for Washington as a picture of poor health.

Sitting on the ballot box in Texas was a brutal game.

Chapter 7

MAKING HIS MARK

The freshman senator from Texas made his first Senate speech in March, railing against President Harry Truman. The speech was one of many delivered during a ten-day "filibuster." This was a favorite tactic by southern senators. They simply "talked to death" any bill or motion they didn't like.

In this instance, under the leadership of Senator Richard B. Russell of Georgia, the southern senators were filibustering against a rule change. It would allow President Truman's Fair Deal legislation to come up for a vote.

Like FDR's New Deal, Truman's Fair Deal angered conservative voters and their congressmen. For one thing, Truman wanted to repeal the Taft-Hartley Act, a law dealing with labor unions. The President's legislative package also included an extension of Social Security, mandatory health insurance, a civil rights program and a minimum wage increase.

Back in Texas, Lyndon knew that most of these Truman measures were unpopular. But he had another reason for making his March speech warning of "a Presidential dictatorship." Purely and simply, Lyndon was seeking the goodwill of Senator Russell. In Lyndon's view, the ex-Georgia governor was the most powerful man in the U.S. Senate.

Lyndon had no intention of being just another freshman senator. He was making his mark swiftly. Swifter, certainly, than any of the other promising new senators—Hubert Humphrey of Minnesota, Estes Kefauver of Tennessee, Paul Douglas of Illinois, and Robert Kerr of Oklahoma. His role in helping Senator Russell to kill Truman's Fair Deal was just one of many fevered activities.

In similar circumstances, a man with less zeal and determination might have faltered. The news about his hotly argued eighty-seven-vote margin over Coke Stevenson had been carried to Washington by the defeated candidate himself. Stevenson wanted a congressional investigation. In the national press, columnists were talking about "Landslide Lyndon" and many unflattering jokes about dirty Texas politics were heard.

But Lyndon was irrepressible. If he met an unfriendly senator, he extended his hand, smiled beamingly, and drawled, "Howdy, I'm Landslide Lyndon."

He requested autographed photos of the other ninety-five senators to hang on his office wall in Suite 231 of the Senate Office Building. Ordinarily, Lyndon wouldn't have been in Suite 231. It had four rooms, and freshman senators usually got only three. But then, while giving the Senate sergeant-at-arms the "Johnson treatment," Lyndon had gotten an extra telephone line, too.

Rather than soft words and cajolery, Lyndon had used harsh words to get his special parking place. It was close to his office. But as Capitol Police Chief Olin Cavness told him, it was reserved for senators with more seniority. "All right,"

Lyndon shouted at the unhappy policeman, "while I'm getting some more seniority, you put a Capitol cop there every morning to guard my space until I get to work!" Remarkably, for reasons never revealed, the chief did just as Lyndon ordered.

The squabble over a parking space proved anew Lyndon's concern about time. He had none to waste. Any congressman who took Washington seriously, who had strong ambitions, found that the capital absorbed time like a sponge.

At one point, Lyndon divided his staff into three shifts, so that the typewriters and mimeograph machines would be running twenty-four hours a day. Crowded into three rooms, his twenty-man staff was expected to handle hundreds of letters and telephone calls daily. There were dozens of visitors, too. Under Lyndon's close supervision, his staffers sent free copies of a Government Printing Office's booklet, *Child Care*, to new parents in Texas. They sent free seeds, newsletters, and speeches to hundreds of thousands of voters. And to any Texas infant named Lyndon, they dispatched a free calf at Lyndon's expense.

Lyndon could never forget he had a selling job to do back in Texas. "Almost exactly one-half of the people who voted in the Democratic primary didn't want me for their senator," he said. "My big job is to get them to change their minds about me." As early as December of 1948, Lyndon was preparing for his re-election, six years away.

If they didn't like the pace—and there were many complaints—Lyndon's staff could only admit that the boss worked just as hard, or harder. Even Lady Bird criticized her husband for his hurry. "Lyndon acts as though there was never going to be a tomorrow," she fussed. Yet there always was.

For Lyndon it usually began about 7 A.M. While still in

bed, he ate breakfast, scanned the *Congressional Record* and the Washington newspapers. Then he shaved with an electric razor.

By 8 A.M., he was telephoning staff members and others furiously. On many days, he handled more than one hundred calls himself. After dressing in the clothes that Lady Bird had laid out, he motored off to pick up his secretary, Mary Rather. "By the time I sat down he was giving me instructions," she remembered. "I learned to keep my notebook outside my purse."

When Lyndon was in town, he could usually be found at 5 P.M. every day at the south end of the Capitol. He was attending meetings of Sam Rayburn's "Board of Education." These social hours were held in the House leader's private lounge, open only to select friends. Many acts of legislative strategy were plotted in this jovial atmosphere.

On occasion, Lyndon and Lady Bird attended one of the endless chain of Washington social events. But usually, Lyndon was working late. He gave little time to such leisurely pursuits as reading novels and watching movies. Once he and several other senators were scheduled to have their pictures taken with one of the country's most popular movie actresses, Lana Turner.

"Who," Lyndon asked vacantly, "is Lana Turner?"

The Democrats placed their eighteen freshman senators on key committees in 1949. Lyndon landed seats on the powerful Armed Services Committee and the Interstate and Foreign Commerce Committee. Within a year or two, both committees would give Lyndon a springboard into the head-lines.

The first opportunity came in June, 1949. It was Truman's

mistake. He shouldn't have nominated Leland Olds, a former minister and journalist, for a third term as chairman of the Federal Power Commission. Olds had angered natural gas producers, from Texas and elsewhere, by deciding to keep natural gas prices low. After much delay, chairman Ed Johnson of the Commerce Committee announced that a subcommittee headed by Lyndon Johnson would hold hearings on the Olds nomination.

They started in late September. From the first, it was obvious that Lyndon intended to use the Olds affair to build goodwill for himself with Texas oilmen. The congressmen couldn't condemn Olds for doing his job. He did that well. But Olds was terribly vulnerable on another count. Twenty years earlier, he had criticized the capitalist system. "Capitalism in the United States is rapidly passing into a stage which has marked the decay of many earlier social orders," he had written.

Lyndon's subcommittee put Olds on the defensive, and he never recovered. Day after day, Lyndon tore into Olds, probing his views and writings as a young man. The subcommittee finally voted 7-to-0 and the full committee 10-to-2 against his confirmation. When the issue reached the Senate floor, Olds was rejected 53-to-15. "Olds was . . . not a Communist," Lyndon had told his colleagues, "but the line he followed, the phrases he used, the causes he espoused, resembled the party line today." Again, Truman's own party had wounded him, and again, Lyndon had worked against his party's President.

Truman made another, and much more serious, mistake in October, 1950. It involved an obscure peninsula in Asia called Korea. At the end of World War II, the tiny country, which had been conquered by Japan, was divided. Half was put under the jurisdiction of Russia and half under that of the United States. Eventually, the country was to be rejoined. But in June of 1950, the Communist-backed North Korean army had invaded the U.S.-controlled South, and Truman had committed U.S. troops to aid the army of the Republic of South Korea.

On October 2, with the North Koreans in flight, Truman ordered Gen. Douglas MacArthur to capture all of the divided country. Clearly, Truman was gambling that neighboring Red China would not interfere. But on November 26, the President learned that he was wrong: 200,000 Chinese soldiers were pouring into North Korea from Manchuria.

On December 12, Lyndon delivered another Senate speech. As he had done during and after World War II, he again called for total mobilization by the U.S. "We are at war not merely with Communist China, but with all the military strength and both the physical and the human resources behind the Iron Curtain," Lyndon warned. "Our primary and immediate goal in this war is survival."

The speech made headlines. But then, Lyndon had already been making headlines with his Preparedness Investigating Subcommittee in the Senate Armed Services Committee. Lyndon hadn't forgotten how Harry Truman had used his war preparedness investigations during World War II for great political gain. Truman, of course, was now President. Now Lyndon saw his chance.

One syndicated columnist wrote, "It is already being said that Lyndon Johnson wants to be President. . . ."

Another step toward achieving that goal came on January 2, 1951. On that occasion, the Senate Democrats met to replace their leaders, wiped out in the 1950 elections. For majority leader, they tapped Ernest McFarland of Arizona.

And for the number-two spot, the majority whip, they unanimously named a senator with only two years' seniority: Lyndon.

The strength of Lyndon's support surprised McFarland. The Arizona senator had never seen such organization.

"Thank the Lord," said Speaker Sam Rayburn, when he heard the news. "Now Lyndon will have something to talk about besides politics!" That was Rayburn's joking reaction to word that Lyndon was buying a ranch west of Austin. It was one that his grandfather had once owned.

It was at the LBJ Ranch, in a new ranch house, that Lyndon sat watching election returns on television the night of November 4, 1952.

The Democrats' Presidential candidate, Governor Adlai Stevenson of Illinois, was being beaten badly by General Dwight Eisenhower, the Republican candidate. But Lyndon was more concerned with an election upset in Arizona. An unknown named Barry Goldwater had upstaged Ernest McFarland. For the second time, in back-to-back elections, the Senate Democrats were without a leader.

Lyndon placed a telephone call to Senator Russell, reaching him in the Federal Building at Winder, Georgia. Cagily, Lyndon suggested to Russell that he run for the Democratic leader's post. "You be the leader and I'll do the work," he said. But Russell, as Lyndon knew he would, declined, preferring his role as head of the southern bloc. Then Russell, as Lyndon also knew he would, suggested that Lyndon run.

During the next few days, the telephone lines out of Johnson City sizzled. Senator Earle Clements of Kentucky was recruited to help line up Senate liberals. Calls went to

Lyndon's cronies like Bob Kerr of Oklahoma, Clint Anderson of New Mexico and Warren Magnuson of Washington. The six new Democratic senators also got calls. Meanwhile, Russell was getting the word to the twenty-two Democratic senators of the southern bloc.

With Russell's backing, Lyndon knew by the first week in December that the job was his. He needed forty-seven votes, and he had far more.

Still, the liberal Democrats weren't giving up on the candidacy of Senator James Murray of Montana. This angered Lyndon. When the liberals, led by Hubert Humphrey of Minnesota and Lester Hunt of Wyoming, finally realized how beaten they were, they tried to bargain. They would back him if he would put two liberals on the Senate Democratic Policy Committee, Humphrey told Lyndon.

Lyndon's answer was prompt. "I don't have to give you anything," he snapped. "I have the votes." He named Earle Clements as the Democratic whip, and then launched the Senate Democrats of the Eighty-third Congress on a strange political sea.

Because of President Eisenhower's tremendous appeal to 1952 voters, the Democrats were now underdogs in both houses. In the Senate, the lineup was 49 Republicans, 47 Democrats and an Independent, Wayne Morse of Oregon. The House had 321 Republicans and 312 Democrats, and an Independent. That meant that both Sam Rayburn, the House Democratic leader, and Lyndon had to think through their dealings with a Republican-controlled government.

They made the decision together. They saw that partisan tempers were high on both sides. The Republicans were back in power for the first time in twenty years, and the Democrats were seething after a vicious defeat. They had been painted by

Republicans as a party of "Crime, Communism, Cronyism, and Korea." The Democrats needed a new image, one of responsibility.

Lyndon told his Senate Democratic colleagues, ". . . if we go forward as positive Americans—and not negative oppositionists—I am convinced that the time is not far distant when the Democratic party will again be in the majority." His decision angered the Senate liberals, anxious to attack the Eisenhower government. They gave Lyndon a new nickname: "Lying-Down Lyndon."

In that respect there was one important issue where Lyndon and many of his Democratic colleagues tried to stay out of the news. That was the infamous McCarthy affair. Lyndon felt that Senator Joseph McCarthy, a Wisconsin Republican, should be left to the Republicans.

In 1950, McCarthy had begun a vicious campaign. He claimed that Communists had invaded the U.S. government. He attacked one public official after another, ruining the reputations of many.

The turning point finally came in late spring of 1954, with thirty-six days of nationally televised hearings. The object of McCarthy's attacks during the hearings was the U.S. Army, but it was McCarthy, not the Army, who was the big loser. After the hearings, the Senate leadership decided it could not permit any more embarrassment from the Wisconsin senator. So Lyndon finally joined Majority Leader William Knowland of California in appointing a special select committee to investigate McCarthy. And the six-man committee suggested censure on two counts.

On December 2, 1954, the entire Senate voted 67 to 22 to condemn McCarthy for bringing "the Senate into dishonor and disrepute."

Even then, realizing that many Texas voters had admired McCarthy, Lyndon felt it politically wise to say a kind word about him. "Joe McCarthy had strength, he had great courage, he had daring," Lyndon said. "There was a quality about the man which compelled respect." Privately, Lyndon wondered why the Republicans had waited so long to move against him.

One reason that Lyndon had paid little heed to the McCarthy affair was that there were other topics on his mind in the summer and fall of 1954.

First, back home, there was a candidate running against him in the '54 Democratic primary. Lyndon had feared that it would be Governor Allan Shivers, who had put together a powerful political machine in Texas. But instead, it was Dudley Dougherty, a rancher and oilman. Dougherty's race created little excitement, so Lyndon decided not to return home to campaign.

He said he was too busy with the affairs of the nation, but actually, he had another goal in mind. If he could help get enough Democrats elected to the Senate, he would become majority leader. And with a Republican President in the White House, he could then contest Adlai Stevenson for control of the Democratic party.

On the night of the election, Speaker Rayburn joined Lyndon in his Washington office until about midnight, keeping track of the Texas voting. Finally, Rayburn left. He was in a foul mood.

"I don't understand Lyndon," he fussed. "He's winning two to one, and yet he stays on the phone to get the results from some piddling little precinct in the Texas Panhandle."

Rayburn was right. At that moment, Lyndon was on the

phone, shouting, "Fifty-seven to forty-three? That's not bad in a box where I just got six votes in 1948."

Lyndon won 3 to 1. And then he hit the road, determined to help elect as many Democratic senators as he could.

Chapter 8

MAJORITY LEADER

It was luridly hot in Wyoming, and sweat sluiced down Lyndon's neck, leaving his collar stained and damp. He was miserable, as anyone could tell. He fidgeted and rolled his eyes impatiently.

The heat was bad, but old Joseph O'Mahoney's speech was much, much worse. Worried by all the hatred stirred up by Senator Joseph McCarthy, the anti-Communist firebrand, O'Mahoney was defending himself. As an attorney, the seventy-eight-year-old former U.S. senator from Wyoming had once represented a man labeled a "subversive" by some. Before a campaign crowd seated in a tabernacle, O'Mahoney had talked of little else for almost an hour.

"Senator!" Lyndon whispered loudly. The people in the front rows looked his way, startled. "Senator," Lyndon said, ignoring the stares, "tell these good voters what you are going to *do* for them when you get back to Washington!"

With Lyndon's help, O'Mahoney won his race, returning to the U.S. Senate after an absence of two years. The other Democrats Lyndon had helped also won, senators like Murray in Montana and Humphrey in Minnesota. But it wasn't until the day after the election that Lyndon knew he had a good chance to be Senate majority leader. Just one man stood in the way. Wayne Morse, the Independent from Oregon.

The outspoken Morse had once denounced Lyndon as "more Republican than Democrat," as "a follower, not a leader." But both Lyndon and Morse realized that this was a good time for forgetting old wounds.

They struck a trade. A key seat on the Senate Foreign Relations Committee for Morse, and for Lyndon, Morse's vote for majority leader. That gave the Democrats 49 votes, the Republicans 47. Thus Lyndon, with his black hair graying and lines deepening in his long face, became the youngest majority leader in Senate history. He was forty-six.

Lyndon's other plan hadn't worked out. Adlai Stevenson still controlled the Democratic party machinery. In December, Paul Butler, an Indiana lawyer, had been elected chairman of the Democratic National Committee. Butler was an avid Stevenson supporter, and, just as frustrating to Lyndon, he was bitterly opposed to Eisenhower.

Butler and most of the liberal Democrats in Congress expected their party leaders to attack the Republican President and his legislative program. But again, as in 1953, the liberal Democrats were disappointed. Lyndon and Speaker Sam Rayburn had no such plans.

For an explanation, the unhappy Democrats got one of Lyndon's homespun stories. "My daddy would gather us kids around the kitchen table when there was a decision to be made," he said gravely. "Daddy would begin with a quotation from the prophet Isaiah: 'Come now, and let us reason together.'" And that, said Lyndon, was good advice for Democrats and Republicans in the Eighty-fourth Congress.

Had Lyndon and Rayburn chosen to, they could have badly weakened the Eisenhower administration. But they were looking at political realities. They didn't think any Democrat could defeat Ike in the 1956 elections. And the people of the United States were reasonably content, with the economy booming and no war. In Lyndon's appraisal, this was no time for bitter partisan battles, especially since the Democrats' control of each house was so slight.

It was, however, time for surgery. His severe backaches had started in December, but Lyndon had postponed any operation until Congress was in session and he was officially the Senate majority leader. Within a few days after being elected to the Senate post, he was in Rochester, Minnesota, at the Mayo Brothers' Clinic, where doctors removed a kidney stone. Slowed by his recuperation, he didn't return to the floor of the Senate until March 8.

The old man in the thick glasses and dark, worn suit occupied the first twenty minutes of Lyndon's time each day on the Senate floor. His name was Walter George. He had come to the Senate in 1922 from Vienna, Georgia. He had a pet parakeet at home, and he had a deep, burnished voice that made him one of the Senate's favorite orators.

Senator George insisted on sitting next to Lyndon's desk on the front row center aisle, and he insisted on being briefed daily by the majority leader.

One of Senator George's favorite comments was, "We must take the *rr*easonable view." Out of George's sight, Lyndon liked to mimic the little senator. Lyndon had a gift for imitating others. Dropping his voice, Lyndon would say, "We must take the *rr*easonable view," and it sounded just like the Vienna sage. Pulling his glasses down on his nose, Lyndon became Senator William Fulbright of Arkansas. Shuffling slowly across the room, he became Senator William Knowland, the minority leader. And he was especially good at imitating a diffident President Eisenhower at a news conference. "Well, no; I have—as a matter of fact, I think—as you state it . . ." Lyndon would say aimlessly, enjoying the laughter of his audience.

But he had less and less time to enjoy himself, especially after returning from his kidney-stone surgery. Lyndon wanted to make a strong showing as majority leader, and two months of the Eighty-fourth Congress had already passed. After briefing Senator George each day, Lyndon would talk with reporters for five minutes, outlining the day's business. At straight-up noon, under Lyndon's ever-heavy hand, the United States Senate went to work.

Speed was what mattered to Lyndon. Speed, and results. To hurry Senate business along, Lyndon personally took charge of even the routine bills. On almost any afternoon, he could get a hundred of these bills passed. He would begin by saying, "I ask unanimous consent that the Senate proceed to the consideration of—" and he would name the bill. With the consent given, he would finish with, "The bill was ordered to a third reading, read the third time, and passed." Then he hurried on to the next bill, and the next.

With the aid of the secretary to the Senate majority, a young man from Pickens, South Carolina, named Bobby Gene Baker, Lyndon could accurately predict how the Senate was going to vote on a bill. If he needed more votes, he would turn Washington upside down to locate absent senators.

One afternoon in June, 1955, he believed that he needed Hubert Humphrey's vote. Learning that Senator Humphrey was on an airliner waiting to land at Washington's National

Airport, he telephoned the control tower. "I want him down quick," Lyndon ordered the controller. "You better be awful sure he's not stacked up there." With Lyndon's aid, Humphrey arrived just in time to vote.

With this kind of ardor, Lyndon could brag to reporters at the end of the first session of the Eighty-fourth Congress: "We passed about 30 per cent more bills in about 30 per cent less time than the Republican Eighty-third Congress. Furthermore, this Senate session tackled important and highly controversial legislation—minimum wage, public housing, Upper Colorado River project, long-range trade program. No one of these bills took longer than three days to pass."

Lyndon's bragging irked the Republicans. A few days earlier, President Eisenhower had gone out of his way at a press conference to chide Lyndon. The Democrats might be passing a lot of bills, Ike said, but there were more than a dozen major bills not enacted yet. The President suggested that Lyndon work a little harder.

This time, Lyndon forgot about the Democratic leaders' "Be Kind to Ike" campaign. He lashed the President fiercely, criticizing Ike's golf, bridge-playing, and many vacations. Lyndon added stingingly, "We are not going to carry out instructions like a bunch of second lieutenants."

The clash drew smiles from Lyndon's friends. They knew that Lyndon was only saying publicly what he often said in private—that he could smash Ike politically if he wanted to. They knew, too, that if he worked any harder, he would kill himself.

Late the afternoon of July 2, the pain struck Lyndon again.

The first attack had hit him in May, during a Senate

debate. The second came on June 18 while his chauffeur, Norman Edwards, was driving him to the Virginia estate of George Brown, Lyndon's Texas contractor friend. And the third was just like the rest. . . .

He was in his limousine with his chauffeur, Norman. They were going to George Brown's. As he had before when the pain hit, Lyndon asked Norman to stop for a Coke, but the carbonated water didn't help his nausea. The pain that gripped his chest was fierce, as if a truck had fallen on him.

At Brown's, Lyndon met Senator Clinton Anderson of New Mexico, who knew what it was like to have a heart attack. "What is it when you hurt right here, Clint?" Lyndon asked feebly, pointing to his chest.

"Does it hurt up and down your left arm, too?" Anderson asked. Lyndon agreed that it did.

"You're having a heart attack!" Anderson replied quickly.

The ambulance came from Bethesda Naval Hospital, and it was there, on the seventeenth floor, that Lyndon began a long recovery from a myocardial infarction—a heart attack of moderately severe nature. A blood clot had blocked a heart artery. To recover, Lyndon needed lots of bed rest and no worries at all.

After several weeks in the hospital, Lyndon flew home to the LBJ Ranch, where he alternately ignored his doctors and took them seriously. Within a week, members of the Johnson staff began to appear from Washington, and Lyndon started telephoning colleagues against the doctors' orders. But he did reduce from 220 pounds to 185 as his doctors requested. He cut his daily caloric intake from 1,500 to 1,200 calories. And he quit his three-packs-a-day smoking habit in favor of chewing gum and low-calorie candy. But before long, the public was far more interested in another heart-attack victim.

On September 24, in Denver, President Eisenhower was felled by a heart attack while on a golfing vacation. Not only did his illness raise doubts about Ike's ability to complete his term, the attack also cast long shadows over the 1956 Presidential nominations, speeding the pulse of every politician of note, whether Democrat or Republican.

If Ike didn't run again, who would be their candidate, the Republicans wondered. "When I get to that bridge I'll jump off it," said GOP National Chairman Leonard Hall, grimly.

The Democrats, like the Republicans, had assumed that Ike would run and win. Now they realized they might be looking at a whole new ball game.

When Lyndon returned in January, the question of the Democratic nomination overshadowed the U.S. Senate. Already, Adlai Stevenson had announced his candidacy, and Estes Kefauver of Tennessee, Averell Harriman of New York, Stuart Symington of Missouri, Albert Gore of Tennessee, and John Kennedy of Massachusetts were making feverish plans.

In one sense, so was Lyndon. Seeking to offset some of the publicity given to Stevenson's November announcement, he made a key campaignlike speech in December at tiny Whitney, Texas. Then in March, a front-page headline appeared in *The New York Times*: A JOHNSON BOOM STARTS IN THE SOUTH. In April, two Texas friends opened an Austin office with "Lyndon Johnson for President Committee" painted on the door.

But in other ways, Lyndon wasn't acting like a true candidate. He didn't seem to have any firm strategy for the Chicago national convention in August. He would lead the fifty-six-man Texas delegation, which was committed to him as a favorite son. But when a *Newsweek* reporter asked him shortly before the convention what he was going to do, Lyndon answered, "I don't know."

Belatedly, Lyndon's interest seemed to pick up. The day before the convention opened, reporters rushed up to Lyndon and Sam Rayburn at the Chicago airport. One reporter told Rayburn that a news ticker had quoted him as having announced his support for Stevenson.

"I haven't said I was for anybody but Lyndon," Rayburn snapped, and he walked briskly away. As usual, Lyndon stayed behind, visiting with newsmen. While waiting for his protégé, Rayburn turned to a friend, "I hate to see Lyndon get bit so hard by the Presidential bug at this stage of the game," Rayburn said, frowning. "Stevenson's got it sewed up."

It was, indeed, Stevenson on the first ballot. And that fall, it was, again, a hale and hearty Eisenhower by a landslide. In the U.S. Senate, despite Ike's massive victory, the lineup was again forty-nine Democrats and forty-seven Republicans.

"I am not a civil rights leader," Lyndon had told reporters testily in March, 1956. And his record easily supported him.

But in 1957, Lyndon realized that his needs had changed. His needs and the nation's. Before, as a senator from a Confederate state, he hadn't dared to speak out in support of Negro causes. To do so would be to invite probable defeat in the next election. Sam Rayburn, speaking in Lyndon's defense, once told reporters, "I'm not sure that a man can be a liberal from Texas." Especially on civil rights, Sam could have added.

So Lyndon had persistently voted against civil rights measures, including an anti-lynching bill in 1940, a measure to eliminate poll taxes in 1940, and bills against segregation in the armed forces in 1942, 1943, and 1945. He had attacked President Truman's 1948 civil rights program as "an effort to set up a police state in the guise of liberty." As late as July, 1956, he was the author of a strategy that killed President Eisenhower's Civil Rights Bill, though some argued that it was weak and deserved to be killed.

But politics, as Douglass Cater wrote in *The Reporter* in September, 1957, "can play a creative as well as a divisive role."

There had been a marked shift of black voters away from the Democratic candidates in 1956. The Black Revolution was under way. There was no longer going to be any denial of the new breed of blacks' insistence on fairer treatment. And there was no denying Lyndon, either. He sought a new political image. He wanted to be seen as a candidate broader than just a senator from Texas, a senator from the South. And what better way was there than to get the first civil rights bill in eighty-two years through the Senate?

Lyndon didn't advertise the fact. He was, in fact, silent about his plan. No one knew exactly what he was going to do when the Eisenhower administration's Civil Rights Bill passed the House on June 18, 1957.

It came to the Senate in the next few weeks, and the scenario that Lyndon authored was little short of brilliant, even in the Senate, which was noted as an arena for brilliant strategies. He knew that he had to prevent a filibuster by southern senators, which would probably kill the bill. To placate the South, he had to chop from the bill its most controversial elements—especially the part giving the U.S. Attorney General the power to seek injunctions to enforce civil rights for blacks.

And that, with his parliamentary skills and his personal appeals, was what he did.

On August 7, Lyndon cast the most important vote of his

career. He joined his Texas colleague, Ralph Yarborough, the two Tennessee senators, and Senator George Smathers of Florida as southerners voting for a civil rights bill. It passed, 72 to 18. If the voters back home rebelled, it could mean political retirement for him, Lyndon realized. He told the Senate as much, just before the vote. "I tell you, out of whatever experience I have," he said slowly, "that there is no political capital in this issue." Then he predicted, "Political ambition which feeds off hatred of the North or hatred of the South is doomed to frustration. There is a compelling need for a solution that will enable all Americans to live in dignity and in unity. This bill is the greatest step toward that objective that has ever been made."

That was probably phrasing it a little too strongly. But the 1957 Civil Rights Bill was a beginning. And so was Sputnik.

This was the Russians' name for the 184-pound satellite launched into orbit by the Soviet Union on October 4, 1957. In this shiny little sphere, roughly the size of a beach ball, Lyndon found another ready-made issue to aid his Presidential campaign hopes.

From all the public clamor about Sputnik, Lyndon knew that the U.S. would have to join the Russians in the space race. Lots of headlines lay ahead, and Lyndon thought a good way to lay claim to them was to start hearings by his Defense Preparedness Subcommittee in the Senate Armed Services Committee.

"We've got to admit frankly and without evasion that the Soviets have beaten us at our own game—daring scientific adventures in the space age," he contended.

The Russians put up a heavier Sputnik II on November 2. On December 2, the U.S. failed in an attempt to launch Vanguard I successfully, and Lyndon fumed, "How long, how long, oh God, how long will it take us to catch up with the Russians' two satellites?" This was a question that he sought to answer with his subcommittee hearings.

In February, 1958, Lyndon put through a new Senate Committee on Aeronautical and Space Sciences, the first new standing Senate committee since 1946. He became its chairman. By this point, he was far and away the nation's leading political voice on the subject of space. It was to be a pet topic with him for the remainder of the Eighty-fifth Congress' second term.

The space issue, in fact, marked a high point in Lyndon's Senate career and Senate power. Never again would he control the Senate quite so completely. So many Democratic congressmen were elected in the November, 1958 races that the whole chemistry of the House and Senate was changed.

"I'd just as soon not have that many Democrats," Speaker Rayburn had muttered before the 1958 election. It was increasingly obvious that the Democrats were going to elect new congressmen in droves. "Believe me," predicted Rayburn, "they'll be hard to handle."

The Democrats ended up with a 283-to-153 lead in the House, and a 65-to-35 lead in the Senate.

And they were, as Rayburn had predicted, hard to handle. For once, so was President Eisenhower. Ike suddenly unholstered his Presidential revolver as he never had in the past six years, and began firing at legislation he didn't like. For bullets, he used his Presidential veto.

The relationship between the Senate and Ike had changed vastly from the time in 1955 when Lyndon had bragged to some of his intimates in the Senate, "I've got the committee chairmen and I could make him sweat." "Him" being the

President, of course. This time, Lyndon was sweating. He was trapped between two implacable camps: the Democratic liberals, for whom he could never do enough; and Eisenhower, from whom he was always wanting too much.

That was, for Lyndon, the story of the Eighty-sixth Congress. It was a "do-nothing" Congress from a Democratic point of view. To the chagrin of Senator John F. Kennedy, who had proposed a milder bill, the Republicans pushed through the Landrum-Griffin Labor Reform Act, which struck hard at the power of labor unions. There were suspicions that Lyndon may not have fought the Landrum-Griffin Act as hard as he could have, perhaps hoping to harm Kennedy's chances for the 1960 Democratic Presidential nomination.

In the early months of the 1960 session, the Eighty-sixth Congress tackled the subject of civil rights, and this time the southerners filibustered. Day after day, night after night, they flailed away at the bill, and for once, Lyndon was bewildered. The filibuster started on February 29; it was still going in mid-March.

Finally, on May 6, a weak civil rights measure went to Eisenhower for his signature. It was a victory for the South.

Lyndon decided the Congress should return in August after the national conventions for a short "rump" session. But this idea, too, was a failure. It fell victim to Presidential aspirations—John F. Kennedy's and Richard M. Nixon's. Both were in the Senate. Both rallied their party members behind them. There was no room for compromise. And that was the name of the Johnson system—compromise. Without it, he was almost, though not quite, just another senator.

It was on this note that Lyndon's congressional career came to an end.

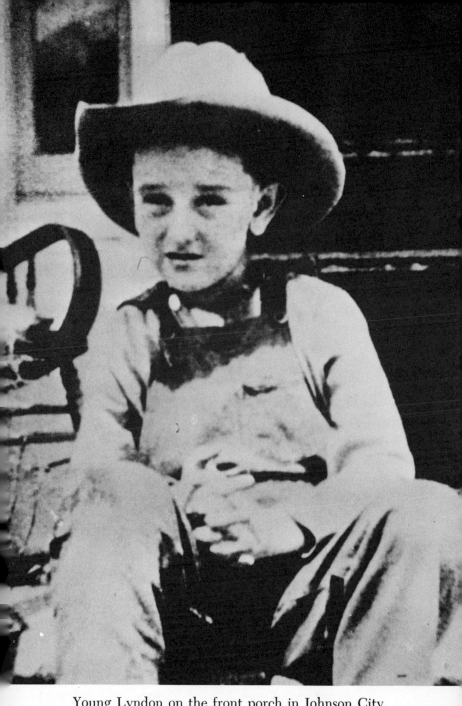

Young Lyndon on the front porch in Johnson City.

Lyndon (*right*) with two of his debate partners
at Southwest Texas State College.

Sam Ealy Johnson, Jr., with his two sons,
Sam Houston (*left*) and Lyndon Baines.

Texas Governor James V. Allred (*center*) and Lyndon welcome FDR to Galveston, May 11, 1937.

Lieutenant Commander Johnson was sent on a fact-finding mission to the Pacific Theater during World War II.

Campaigning for the Senate, 1941.

The *Johnson City Windmill* took Lyndon's 1948 Senate campaign to every part of Texas.

Majority Leader Johnson confers with Senate colleagues.

Campaigning with Kennedy in 1960.

Vice-President Johnson meets a camel driver in Pakistan.

November 22, 1963. The new President takes the oath of office.

On the telephone—a characteristic pose.

Four black leaders—Roy Wilkins, James Farmer, Martin Luther King, and Whitney Young—confer with the President in the Oval Office.

Greeting soldiers in Vietnam.

March 31, 1968. "I shall not seek, and I will not accept, the nomination of my party...."

Vietnam war protesters at the Pentagon, October 21, 1967. (*left*)

Lady Bird, Lynda, LBJ, and Luci with her husband Pat Nugent and their baby Patrick Lyndon.

General Ky of South Vietnam was one of the many visitors to the ranch on the Pedernales.

A briefing session with candidate Nixon, August 1968.

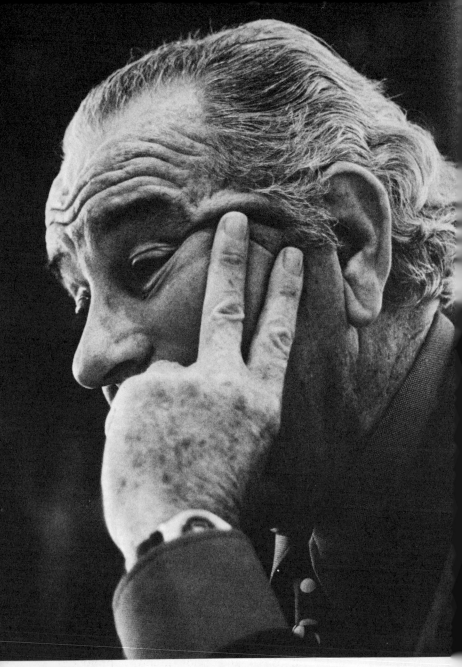

January 6, 1973. One of the last photographs of LBJ.

Chapter 9

SHORTFALL

Did Lyndon seriously run for President in 1960? If he did, did he *really* understand what Presidential politics was all about?

The answer to both questions is no, not until it was too late.

The fault was mostly his. Numerous friends, political donors, and loyal campaign strategists urged him many times to get his Presidential hopes in order. James H. Rowe, Jr., the New Deal strategist, was one. This was the year for a southerner like Johnson to win, Rowe argued. But Lyndon, plagued with doubts, said that he wasn't a candidate.

Devoted friends like Speaker Sam Rayburn ignored Lyndon's answer. One of Rayburn's ambitions was to see his protégé elected President. In October, 1959, Rayburn set up an unofficial "Johnson for President" committee. Soon after, a Johnson headquarters was opened in Austin. On Wall Street, financiers like Edwin Weisl and Eliot Janeway promoted Lyndon's candidacy. And in the South and Far West, Lyndon's name was kept before the public by small groups of boisterous

Texans who traveled widely, using the slogan "All the Way with LBJ."

But officially, Lyndon's "no" was unshakable. "I don't want to get a bug in my mouth that I can't swallow," he had told an acquaintance in early 1959. "I don't have the disposition, the training, or the temperament for the Presidency." So Lyndon's candidacy moved on without him, and its leaders miscalculated badly.

What his advisers expected was a pro-Johnson union of southerners, old New Dealers, and congressmen who could be influenced by Lyndon and Speaker Sam. The Johnson staffers believed that Lyndon would get the votes of all the southern delegates, plus many western delegates and some from the North and East, where the New Dealers still had some influence. Walter Jenkins, one of Lyndon's personal aides, explained why he expected some help from California. "The Senator worked out there as a young man for a couple of years—running an elevator in an office building," Jenkins recalled.

But there was a fatal flaw in this strategy. That was the fact that most of the people they were counting on couldn't deliver the delegates. In Arizona, for example, they were depending on aging Senator Carl Hayden to control that state's delegation. But it was easily stolen for John Kennedy by Rep. Stewart Udall. The same thing happened in Colorado, where the pro-Johnson man was Senator Edwin Johnson. The scene was repeated in Montana, Iowa, New York, and Connecticut, all believed to be controlled by pro-Johnson senators. Instead, the delegations from these states went to Kennedy.

The unexpected Kennedy successes were signs that a potent new force had entered American politics. A new breed of political operator, a new political generation, was coming to power.

These newcomers were pragmatists at heart. They favored action, innovation, and progressivism over seniority, traditional loyalties, and provincialism. Robert Kennedy, the thirty-one-year-old chief of staff for his older brother's campaign, was one of the new breed. So were Kenneth P. O'Donnell, thirty-six, and Pierre Salinger, thirty-five, both members of the Kennedy "Irish Mafia," as the senator's personal staff was called. These men symbolized what historian-journalist Theodore H. White has labeled one of the sharpest breaks in American political history. It was like the 1850s, said White, when the Clay-Calhoun-Webster generation gave way to younger men.

Thus, as the spring of 1960 turned into summer, a tide of youthful, yet skillful, political operators got ready for a trip to California. The Democratic National Convention would be held in Los Angeles in early July. Meanwhile, Lyndon continued to fiddle in the concert hall that he loved and knew best, the U.S. Senate. He felt safe there, safe and secure, wise and responsible. He was leaving it to Senator Kennedy and his Young Turks to flit around the country, politicking.

Instead, Lyndon said, he was nurse-maiding important legislation like bills for increased public housing, a boost in minimum wages, medical aid to the aged, subsidies for new school construction—legislation that the Democratic candidate would need to campaign on that fall. "This country can't stand, the party can't stand, the Senate can't stand having three active Presidential candidates in the Senate—of whom one is the majority leader," he insisted.

The other two? Kennedy and Hubert Humphrey. They had been slugging it out all spring in the Presidential primaries. On May 10, they met again, this time in West Virginia. There Kennedy again won easily, a hint that perhaps the 1960 Democratic nominee had, for practical purposes, already been chosen.

Lyndon, at least, got the message. It was no longer smart, he realized, to be competing for delegates with John Kennedy, Stuart Symington, Adlai Stevenson, and the early also-rans (Humphrey dropped out after West Virginia). The only hope now for the Johnson-for-President movement was to stop John Kennedy's early nomination. In case of a deadlock, Lyndon calculated, perhaps he would be a compromise choice.

So he quickly scheduled several tours—and ordered a set of contact lenses. He hosted the press more frequently and began to encourage his backers. He pressured numerous governors and senatorial candidates for support, using reward-and-punishment tactics as he did in the Senate. At the last minute, in a stunning maneuver, he and Bobby Baker put together a daring plan. That plan was to call the Senate back to Washington *after* the states' nominating conventions. It was believed that this strategy would give the Majority Leader added influence in Los Angeles.

On July 5, just five days before the Democratic National Convention opened, Lyndon announced that he was, after all, a serious candidate. After that, an army of candidates, staffers, delegates, newspeople, and various hangers-on trooped off to California, where a confident and superbly organized John F. Kennedy won the nomination on the first ballot. Kennedy collected 806 votes. Lyndon got 409, Symington 86, Adlai Stevenson 79½, and all the others 140½.

The two top vote-getters were both U.S. senators, but there the similarities ended. Kennedy was forty-three and

Lyndon fifty-two. Kennedy was an Irish Catholic from Massachusetts and Lyndon was a southern Protestant. Kennedy was a charming, quick-witted orator and Lyndon was a roaring, homespun, high-pitched arguer. Kennedy's strengths were highly visible in his handsome looks, decisive mien, and skilled aides, while Lyndon's power was mostly hidden in the hallowed ways and means of the U.S. Senate. As the campaign had progressed, each had insulted the other, with Lyndon's barbs more pointed than Kennedy's.

This is why the events that followed quickly on the heels of John Kennedy's nomination shocked just about everyone, including Kennedy's own brother, Robert.

Lady Bird's gentle shaking roused Lyndon from a deep slumber in Suite 7334 of the Biltmore Hotel. At 8:35 A.M., Senator Kennedy was on the telephone.

For a man who had been selected to run for President only the night before, Kennedy was getting an early start. But there was still serious work in Los Angeles for the Democratic party. A Vice-Presidential candidate was yet to be selected.

Lyndon listened for a moment, spoke briefly, then hung the receiver up. He felt Lady Bird's soft gaze on his face as he told her that Kennedy was coming to their suite at 9:30.

"I know he's going to offer the Vice-Presidency, and I hope you won't take it," she said.

Yet her voice lacked commitment. Lyndon knew she had worried for years about the pressures of the majority leader's post on his health. And, certainly, the Vice-President had fewer pressures. Early in U.S. history, John Adams had termed the job "the most insignificant office that ever the invention of man contrived." Thomas Marshall, Woodrow Wilson's Vice-

President, complained that he had nothing to do. As Vice-President Lyndon might even get home to dinner on time occasionally.

While still in his pajamas, he began issuing orders and placing telephone calls. One went to his boyhood friend, Rep. Homer Thornberry, who had won Lyndon's old 10th District of Texas seat in 1948.

Swiftly, Lyndon broke the news of Kennedy's pending visit to the man he first knew as a page boy in the Texas Capitol. Later, Lyndon learned that Thornberry was in the bathroom with his face lathered for his morning shave when the call reached him.

"Yes, Lyndon," Thornberry replied.

"He may offer me the Vice-Presidential nomination."

"Yes, Lyndon," the congressman said again.

"What do you think I should say?"

"Why, Lyndon, I wouldn't touch it with a ten-foot pole," Thornberry answered.

"But what will I tell Jack?"

Said Thornberry, "Tell Jack anything you want, but don't take it."

Thornberry's attitude came as no surprise to Lyndon, who knew that many of his southern friends would want him to decline the Vice-Presidential candidacy. He would have more power, they would insist, if he remained in the Senate. Or they would say that if he accepted and the Kennedy-Johnson ticket lost, his political career would be destroyed. Others would object to Kennedy's religion. A few would call the very idea of running with a "northern liberal" treasonous to the Old South.

Within a few minutes, Lyndon was surprised suddenly to hear Thornberry's voice again.

"Lyndon, I've been thinking this over," the congressman

blurted. "I was wrong. You ought to take the Vice-Presidency."

Not ready at this point to offer any firm clues to what he was thinking, Lyndon replied, "But, Homer, what'll I tell Mister Sam?"

The night before, unhappy at the defeat of his protégé by the Kennedy forces, Speaker Sam had telephoned to caution Lyndon against accepting the Vice-Presidency. Lyndon had promised not to accept an offer without checking further with him.

At 10:05, delayed by the hectic activities going on in his suite, Kennedy finally arrived, and he and Lyndon immediately went into conference. He thanked the Texas senator for a warm congratulatory telegram, which Lyndon had started writing the night before when the voting reached "Iowa."

Then he moved to more serious business. In his rapid eastern speech, Kennedy told Lyndon that his vast experience made him better qualified than he, Kennedy, to be President. But a southerner, Kennedy said, couldn't be elected. He added, however, that many of the party's top leaders wanted Lyndon Johnson for Vice-President. He, too, had thought it over and he wanted Lyndon as his running mate. Would he accept?

Lyndon said he needed a little time to think, to counsel with his political allies in the South and to talk with Lady Bird. Kennedy said he would call in a few hours, and they split up, each aware that they had set in motion a political chess game of enormous proportions.

The fury erupted almost at once.

One element of the Democratic party—the big-city leaders—favored Lyndon for Vice-President. Another segment, the South, was split, some leaders for and some against.

But the third group, the labor leaders, were totally and bitterly against the idea. They remembered all of Lyndon's anti-labor votes, and they made their views on the matter clear to John Kennedy.

While Kennedy and his staff sought opinions about making Lyndon a firm and public offer, Lyndon weighed the opinions of his friends about joining the Kennedy ticket. He reached Speaker Rayburn, and while Sam's opinion would later change, it hadn't yet. When Lyndon put through a call to old Cactus Jack Garner in Uvalde, Texas, the former Vice-President supported John Adams' view. "I'll tell you, Lyndon," shouted Garner, "the Vice-Presidency isn't worth a pitcher of warm spit."

The noon hour passed, and the bitter debating continued. Confusion packed the steamy, airless corridors outside the Kennedy and Johnson suites, where reporters waited for the final word.

As the minutes ticked off, the confusion grew worse. Kennedy called Lyndon and read a copy of a statement announcing a Kennedy-Johnson ticket. Lyndon, assured that Kennedy really wanted him, agreed to accept. But a few minutes later, Bobby Kennedy arrived at the Johnson suite, warning of a possible nasty floor fight and wondering if Lyndon might want to withdraw. Hearing this, Lyndon exploded.

It was all a mistake. Within minutes, John Kennedy was making his announcement that he had offered Lyndon a place on the Democratic ticket. A few more minutes and Lyndon was announcing that he had accepted.

That night, House Majority Leader John McCormack and Governor LeRoy Collins of Florida, the convention chairman, teamed up to thwart a bitter floor fight over Lyndon's nomination. When McCormack called for a voice rather than a state-by-state vote, Collins put the McCormack question to the floor. The boos were as loud as the ayes, but Collins announced: ". . . Senator Lyndon B. Johnson of Texas has been nominated for the Vice-Presidency of the United States by acclamation."

Two weeks later the Republicans met in Chicago to nominate Richard M. Nixon and Henry Cabot Lodge for President and Vice-President.

For the next four months, Lyndon ignored insults from Texans and other southerners angry at his joining with Kennedy. There was, instead, much work to do. In Los Angeles, Kennedy had received only 9½ votes from the South in getting the nomination, and so Lyndon's role in wooing the Old Confederacy was crucial.

With Lady Bird at his side, Lyndon's most colorful campaigning came in October. For days, the Johnson party rolled through the South on an eleven-car train, stopping at every crossroads. It was called the "LBJ Victory Special," but reporters quickly dubbed the train the "Cornpone Special." In tiny Culpepper, Virginia, Lyndon delivered perhaps the most famous line of the '60 campaign: "What did Richard Nixon ever do for Culpepper?"

In all, Lyndon and his campaigners traveled 3,500 miles on the LBJ Victory Special. But it was what an angry mob of arch-Republicans did in Dallas, Texas, that may have tipped the election decisively toward the Kennedy-Johnson ticket. The Dallas incident outraged many southerners and put Lyndon in a new light with many northerners. For in the lobby of a Dallas hotel, a hostile right-wing crowd insulted and spat at Lyndon and Lady Bird, creating a uniquely ugly scene that was viewed on national television.

Four days later, the nation went to the polls. The Kennedy-Johnson ticket won twenty-three states with 303 electoral votes and the Richard Nixon-Henry Cabot Lodge ticket won twenty-six states with 219 electoral votes. The popular vote was much closer. Kennedy-Johnson won 49.7 per cent, and Nixon-Lodge 49.6 per cent. Close, yes, but the Democrats had won and Lyndon was, as the cliché goes, a heartbeat away from the Presidency.

For two years and ten months, Lyndon operated in the shadow of power while holding little power himself. It was a terribly difficult role for him, and many problems arose. There were conflicts with the Kennedy staff when he was at home, and there were conflicts with the Foreign Service and the State Department when he was abroad, representing the U.S. on his many trips.

His travels were the highlight of his years as Vice-President. He made eleven different tours outside the U.S., far more than any other Vice-President before him. The most important trip came in August, 1961, to reassure West Berliners that the U.S. would defend them from Communist aggression. The trip that the public remembered best was the one on which he met Bashir Ahmad, the Pakistani camel driver. At Lyndon's invitation, Ahmad later visited the Johnsons at the LBJ Ranch in a highly publicized event.

On the domestic scene, Lyndon served important roles in only two areas—enforcing equal opportunity for workers among government contractors and encouraging the nation's space program.

He and Kennedy were never close. As the '64 election drew nearer and nearer, there was much speculation that Kennedy would drop Lyndon in favor of a new Vice-President. Kennedy denied the possibility, and he was still denying it when he and Lyndon came to Dallas one fateful November day.

Chapter 10

DALLAS

"The cars are ready."

"All right, then let's move out."

On that signal, a crowd surged through the side doors of Parkland Hospital in Dallas, Texas, hurrying toward two unmarked police cruisers, motors idling. A lanky, dark-suited man with a white flower in his lapel ducked into the rear seat of one car, following the orders of a U.S. Secret Service agent. The man heard the agent add: "Keep down below the windows." It was 1:26 P.M. It was Friday, the 22nd of November, 1963.

The Secret Service was taking every precaution, fearing more attacks. The agents even ordered the man's wife into the second car, putting her in added danger. But Lady Bird approved. The grim-faced little woman—dressed simply, a string of pearls adorning her firm neck—was to serve as a decoy. If there were other attackers, it was hoped the assassins would fire at her, not at her husband.

"Let's go," shouted the Secret Service agent called "Dagger." He was Rufus W. Youngblood, and he was assigned to Lyndon. In Texas this afternoon, Youngblood wanted to put great distances between the man he guarded and that horrible scene in downtown Dallas. On Elm Street less than an hour before, President Kennedy had been shot.

Thirteen minutes ago, in the emergency room at Parkland Hospital, Lyndon had learned how unbelievable it all was.

John Kennedy was no longer alive.

Safety for Johnson lay at Love Field, an airport just three miles away. Two blue-and-white Boeing 707s were parked there, one beside the other. *Air Force One* was the President's and Aircraft 86970, the Vice-President's. *Air Force One* was a "little White House," with everything for a President to run his country swiftly and safely.

The Kennedy-Johnson tour of Texas had started the day before in San Antonio. Afterwards came Houston, Fort Worth, then Dallas. The crowds had been fantastic—right to the end. In coming to Texas, Kennedy and Johnson had been testing the state's political waters. Kennedy's popularity had dropped, especially in the South, and he was worried about the 1964 election.

But that was, with such numbing speed, now history.

On this autumn afternoon, Lyndon Johnson put the '64 election out of his mind. He dismissed thoughts of friendly crowds, of opinion polls, and of the situation in the South. His thoughts were for his country and his duties in the days ahead. Back in the nation's capital, in Washington, he knew there were mountains of decisions to be made, decisions only *he* could make. The days would be long and the nights somber. But he must rise above his shock and grief to reassure a Congress, a nation, a world, that a strong new leader had arisen to replace the fallen one.

For fifty-five-year-old Lyndon Johnson—a man whom many viewed with suspicion as a "born politician"—was now the thirty-sixth President of the United States.

For the short ride to Love Field, Mr. Johnson stayed jammed down in his seat. It was not comfortable. At six feet, three inches, his gangling legs were cramped. But he approved of the Secret Service's safeguards. He was wondering if Kennedy's murder pointed to an international Communist conspiracy. He wondered if Kennedy's assassin was lurking out there, waiting for a clear shot at *him*.

During the brief drive, Agent Youngblood talked occasionally into the short-wave radio dangling from his shoulder. His coat was unbuttoned, so he could quickly get at his gun. Once, en route to the airport, he reached for it suddenly when a delivery truck swooped in front of the motorcade.

The Secret Service, terribly stunned at President Kennedy's murder, could be proud of the way Agent Youngblood had performed on Elm Street, protecting the Vice-President. The agent had shoved Johnson to the floor and hovered over him, head up, eyes vigilant.

At the wheel of the Johnson car, the driver, a Texas highway patrolman, pushed fiercely against the accelerator and steered the rented Lincoln convertible out onto a nearby freeway. Within seconds, frightened and confused, they were racing down the concrete at eighty miles an hour.

The messages on Youngblood's radio said that Lancer (the code name for Mr. Kennedy) was hurt. Dagger (that was Youngblood) was ordered to cover Volunteer (Mr. Johnson). Two agents each from Halfback and Varsity (the two Secret Service cars) were also being assigned to Mr. Johnson. Youngblood requested a sixth agent, if available, for Victoria

(Mrs. Johnson). Lady Bird and Senator Ralph Yarborough of Texas also were riding in the Johnson car.

The code names puzzled Yarborough. "What *is* it?" he shouted. But there was no answer.

Even after Youngblood spoke briefly to Mr. Johnson, the Vice-President still knew very little. "An emergency exists," the agent shouted in Mr. Johnson's ear. "When we get to the hospital the two of us are going in fast and not joining anybody else."

The stunned Johnson nodded, beginning to suspect the worst. After several sharp turns, they braked to a stop at the hospital.

Youngblood and another Secret Service agent, Emory Roberts, hustled Mr. Johnson through the emergency doors. They rushed him through a ward and into a treatment area screened by white sheets. There, in Booth 13 in Minor Medicine, the Vice-President received the terrible news that the President had been shot, and it looked bad, very bad. Governor John Connally of Texas had been hit, too. No one knew who else was marked for murder. No one knew if the shooting was the work of a conspiracy, or just one man.

At 1:13 P.M., Special Assistant Kenneth O'Donnell of the Kennedy staff brought the confirming word.

"The President is dead, sir."

Mr. Johnson told his wife and an aide named Cliff Carter that they must go quickly. "Make a note of the time," he ordered. He had added, speaking in muted tones, that as they left they must try to attract very little attention.

En route to Love Field, that was still the plan. The police cruisers used no sirens, no flashing lights. The loudest sounds were the growlings of those powerful souped-up motors as the police cars roared away from each signal light. The cars' occupants, lost in their own shattered feelings, scarcely noticed.

In his memoirs, *The Vantage Point*, Mr. Johnson said that the seven minutes spent between Parkland Hospital and Love Field were as crucial as any in his life.

. . . In spite of my sense of personal loss and deep shock, I knew I could not allow the tide of grief to overwhelm me. . . . I realized, ready or not, new and immeasurable duties had been thrust upon me. There were tasks to perform that only I had the authority to perform. A nation stunned, shaken to its very heart, had to be reassured that the government was not in a state of paralysis. I had to convince everyone everywhere that the country would go forward, that the business of the United States would proceed.

In those seven minutes, Lyndon Johnson took control. By the time the police cars reached Love Field, it was Mr. Johnson, not Agent Youngblood, who was giving orders. Dallas Police Chief Jesse Curry was driving the lead car and he headed directly for the ramp at *Air Force One.*

The Johnson party dashed up the steps. The pilot, Col. James Swindal, had already disconnected the ground air conditioning, thinking that the plane would be taking off. That was an error, as everyone on board realized immediately. Quickly, the inside of the big plane heated up like a Turkish bath.

Some of the *Air Force One* crew and the Kennedy staff were watching newscaster Walter Cronkite on CBS-TV. From Dallas there was a news flash. At Parkland Hospital, Malcolm Kilduff, assistant White House press secretary, had just told newsmen: "President John F. Kennedy died at approximately one o'clock Central Standard Time today here in Dallas." CBS had a few other details. The fatal shots had been fired from a high-powered rifle high in a school-book warehouse overlooking Elm Street. Police had a suspect and were looking for him. The whereabouts of the Vice-President was not known.

The "Vice-President," the newscaster said. But that was an error. The U.S. Constitution is not totally clear on how and when a Vice-President replaces a fallen President—or even *if* he replaces him permanently. But most legal authorities and high political figures agree that Lyndon Johnson became President at the moment John Kennedy died. (The bookkeepers at the U.S. Treasury Department upped Mr. Johnson's salary from $35,000 to $100,000 at 1 P.M., Dallas time.)

Mr. Johnson was now in command of the country, and he wanted to make it official.

"Now," said Mr. Johnson, "what about the oath?"

The oath of office for the President is in the U.S. Constitution. Every school library in Dallas had a copy, and every law library, but for a few moments no one could remember where to find the words that the President sought. That included the congressmen aboard *Air Force One*, the new President's staff members, even U.S. Attorney Barefoot Sanders in the Federal Building in downtown Dallas. So Johnson reluctantly decided to call Robert Kennedy, the U.S. Attorney General, who had learned of his brother's assassination only minutes before.

The Attorney General, at his Hickory Hill home in Virginia, listened to all of Mr. Johnson's questions. To some of them he didn't respond. But to Mr. Johnson's question about who could swear him in, Kennedy replied, "I'll be glad to find out and call you back."

While Robert Kennedy was checking with his deputy

attorney general, Nicholas Katzenbach, there was a dispute at Parkland Hospital.

Dr. Earl Rose, the Dallas County medical examiner, said Kennedy's body could not be moved, not until after an autopsy. That was Texas law, Rose said. The Kennedy aides asked that this requirement be waived, Rose said no, and for nearly forty minutes, this hard-headed Texas pathologist had his way. By the time the hearse with John Kennedy's body reached Gate 28 at Love Field, and the heavy casket was placed aboard *Air Force One*, it was 2:15.

"Should we get airborne?" inquired Brig. Gen. Godfrey McHugh, Air Force aide to the late President. They should, agreed Presidential aide O'Donnell and Maj. Gen. Chester V. Clifton, military aide to Mr. Kennedy. But the Kennedy leaders were ignorant of one important fact: Lyndon Johnson was aboard *Air Force One*. He would give the order to leave, and no one else.

The President and Mrs. Johnson entered the tail compartment of *Air Force One*. Mrs. Kennedy was sitting on the bed, her gloves, suit, and stockings caked with the late President's blood.

"Oh, Jackie," Mrs. Johnson said, "you know, we never even wanted to be Vice-President and now, dear God, it's come to this."

Mr. Johnson mentioned the swearing-in.

"What's going to happen?" Mrs. Kennedy asked quietly.

Mr. Johnson replied, "I've arranged for a judge—an old friend of mine, Judge Hughes—to come."

Federal Judge Sarah T. Hughes, a Kennedy appointee, was at home when Sanders, the U.S. Attorney, phoned. She told him that it would take about ten minutes to drive her small sports car to Love Field.

Aboard the plane, Mr. Johnson issued invitations to the ceremony. A few persons in the Kennedy party responded, believing that Attorney General Kennedy had suggested the Dallas swearing-in. (Later, Kennedy said he did not remember this suggestion.) About thirty people crowded into *Air Force One*'s cramped forward compartment.

One of those was Mrs. Kennedy. Mr. Johnson called out to her, "This is one of the saddest moments of my life."

Judge Hughes, her hands shaking, held a three-by-five-inch index card. On it was written the oath of office, which had been phoned from Washington by Deputy Attorney General Katzenbach. The late President's official photographer was standing on a chair, one camera in hand and another hanging around his neck.

Judge Hughes, her voice breaking, started, "I do solemnly swear—"

"Just a minute, Judge!"

Larry O'Brien, a Kennedy special assistant, had interrupted. It was traditional that a President take the oath with his hand on a Bible. An *Air Force One* crew member had found something that looked like a Bible. It was John Kennedy's personal missal, used for the Catholic Mass. O'Brien took it out of its white box and handed it to Judge Hughes.

At 2:38 P.M., in a twenty-eight-second ceremony, Johnson repeated the oath of office after Judge Hughes: "I do solemnly swear . . . that I will faithfully execute the office of President of the United States . . . and will to the best of my ability, preserve, protect and defend the Constitution of the United States." Judge Hughes added, "So help me God."

"So help me God," Mr. Johnson said softly.

The moment that everyone awaited had come. It was official. The President turned to Lem Johns, a Secret Service agent. "Let her roll," he ordered. Judge Hughes, Police Chief Curry and the photographer, Cecil Stoughton, hurried to get off the plane.

Within minutes, Col. Swindal pulled back on the throttle of *Air Force One.* At 2:47 P.M., in a climb almost as steep as a salute, the silvery craft departed Dallas. Its flight path: Texarkana, Memphis, Nashville . . . Washington.

To weather the days ahead, the new President from Texas would need every skill and bit of wisdom that he had gained during twenty-six and a half years in the political arena. As Mrs. Johnson had said, this was what it had come down to.

Chapter 11

"LET US CONTINUE"

It is a seven-minute flight from Andrews Air Force Base to the south lawn of the White House, where the Presidential helicopters land. Before boarding, President Johnson faced a battery of microphones and solemnly read a fifty-seven-word statement to the 3,000 persons present. It ended, "I ask for your help—and God's."

After entering the helicopter, the President relaxed for a few moments. Deep emotions swirled within him. He spoke of Mrs. Kennedy's bravery and poise, of the red roses in her lap, her blood-stained clothes. Then, looking up, he said that the government must go forward. One by one, he questioned three high-ranking officials who were riding with him. They were George Ball, Undersecretary of State; Robert McNamara, Secretary of Defense; and McGeorge Bundy, special assistant to the President for national security. Were there any urgent matters that he must act on at once?

Each man, speaking to Mr. Johnson in turn, said there were none.

The new President, now in office slightly more than five

hours, must have been relieved. There were tensions enough. Six members of the Kennedy Cabinet were away from Washington, all of them aboard a Presidential jet airliner returning from an aborted flight to the Far East. Never before had so many Cabinet members been out of the country at one time, something Mr. Johnson would prohibit in the future.

On the President's mind, too, was the rivalry between the Kennedy party and the Johnson party. After the landing at Andrews AFB, it had flared again. The Kennedys, wishing to follow their family custom of staying close together during times of crisis, had hurried off *Air Force One* with John Kennedy's body, leaving Mr. Johnson behind. While angered at the snub, Mr. Johnson did nothing to interfere. As he later said, "The aura of Kennedy is important to all of us."

There was weariness in his eyes and the strain showed on his face. But Mr. Johnson's motorlike mind and his shrewd political instincts were working double time.

His first priority, the President realized, was to establish "the right to govern." He had to inspire confidence in the people, demonstrating that they could trust him as a leader. All Presidents must do this, of course. But as Mr. Johnson later wrote in *The Vantage Point*, "I suffered another handicap, since I had come to the Presidency not through the collective will of the people but in the wake of tragedy. I had no mandate from the voters."

To receive the people's confidence, Mr. Johnson knew that the change in Chief Executives must be as orderly and smooth as possible, given the murder of a President. That was his second priority: to create a sense of continuity. That's where the "Kennedy aura" was important. Mr. Johnson knew that the memories, goals, ideals, and the staff of the slain

President were needed if the country's heartbeat was to continue without a skip.

On that short helicopter trip to the White House, the new President appealed to McNamara, Bundy, and Ball to stay at their jobs. All other high-level Kennedy staffers were to hear the same plea in the next few hours. "I need you more than *he* did," Mr. Johnson told one Kennedy official after another.

Many persons received personal messages from the President during the first hours after the Dallas tragedy. Walking from the White House to the Vice-President's suite, No. 274, in the nearby Executive Office Building, he quickly began placing telephone calls. He talked to former Presidents Truman and Eisenhower. He tried to get Herbert Hoover, but the eighty-nine-year-old ex-President had already gone to bed. Mr. Johnson left a message.

There were calls, too, to Senator Ted Kennedy, Senator Richard Russell, Speaker John McCormack, Supreme Court Justice Arthur Goldberg, FBI Director J. Edgar Hoover and Sargent Shriver, director of the Peace Corps and a Kennedy brother-in-law.

The first visitors that night were Senator William Fulbright and Ambassador Averell Harriman. After they left, Mr. Johnson thoughtfully penned short notes to the Kennedy children, Caroline and John, Jr. Before leaving for his home, The Elms, Johnson had also visited briefly with congressional leaders of both parties. He asked for their support. All of them, including Senator Everett Dirksen, the Republican minority leader, pledged their cooperation. Only then, at 9:42 P.M., did the tired President get into a limousine with four of his aides, Jack Valenti, Bill Moyers, Cliff Carter, and Horace Busby.

Even at The Elms, Mr. Johnson couldn't leave the

telephone alone. He called another long-time adviser, attorney
Abe Fortas. He also called Keith Funston, president of the
New York Stock Exchange. All in all, it was the beginning of
an incredible thirty days for Mr. Johnson, for Washington, for
the world. It was later estimated that the new President talked
with 3,000 persons during the first month in office.

He talked to the chief policy-making officials at State and
Defense, updating himself on the Vietnam problem and
defense needs.

He talked to the ninety-five heads of state and other
world leaders—England's Sir Alec Douglas-Home, Germany's
Ludwig Erhard, the Soviet Union's Anastas Mikoyan, Ethio-
pia's Haile Selassie—who came to the Kennedy funeral.

With Mrs. Kennedy at his side, he personally reassured
ambassadors from many Latin American countries of his
interest in the Kennedy administration's Alliance for Progress.

He talked to all of the Washington-based foreign ambassadors, to thirty-five governors, to farm leaders, labor leaders,
civil rights leaders, business leaders, editors and publishers,
reporters and commentators. He addressed the nation twice,
and the United Nations General Assembly once.

"But I didn't just talk," Mr. Johnson wrote in *The
Vantage Point*. "I listened carefully to what my visitors had to
say. After I had listened, I always returned to my basic theme:
People must put aside their selfish aims in the larger cause of
the nation's interest."

During these first thirty days in office, the President said
he averaged no more than four or five hours' sleep a night. And
he couldn't remember a single instance where he had time to
go off by himself, to forget the rigors of the job, and just relax.

But evidence began to appear early in that thirty-day

span that Lyndon Johnson's one-man campaign to keep the national confidence up was going to be successful. On Monday, November 25, the New York Stock Exchange experienced a tremendous rally. The averages went up 32.03 points, the biggest one-day rally in the history of the Dow-Jones industrial stock index. It was a good sign.

An address to Congress, the budget, a reduction in taxes, and civil rights.

These were Mr. Johnson's primary concerns following John Kennedy's burial in Arlington National Cemetery the afternoon of Monday, November 25. The first priority went to the speech to a joint session of Congress, which was two days away. It would probably be the most important speech Mr. Johnson would ever deliver.

Originally, the speech was scheduled for Tuesday, but Robert Kennedy objected. He felt the date was too close to his brother's burial. So it was not until Wednesday that Mr. Johnson, accompanied by three long-time Kennedy staffers, went to Capitol Hill. At 12:30 that afternoon, using a speech largely written by Ted Sorensen of Kennedy's staff and Abe Fortas, an old friend of Lyndon's, the President staked out his claim on a future that rightfully belonged to John Kennedy.

The President made that clear. "All I have I would have given gladly not to be standing here today," were his opening words.

He went on to pledge his support for the Kennedy programs. That included military aid to South Vietnam and West Berlin. It meant continued foreign aid to many Asian, African, and Latin American countries. It signaled a push for new civil rights laws and a tax-cut bill. Said Mr. Johnson, "No act of ours could more fittingly continue the work of President Kennedy than the earliest passage of the tax bill for which he fought all this long year."

The speech, interrupted by applause thirty-two times, was splendid. Mr. Johnson talked slowly, with dignity. He didn't wave his arms and shout like the wagon-bed orator that he often had been. He said it was a "time for action," a phrase which he later used as the title of a book. He borrowed a Kennedy phrase—"Let us begin," and counseled, "Let us continue."

In places of honor, sitting with Lady Bird, were three highly symbolic figures. One was Governor Carl Sanders of Georgia, a representative of the South. Another was Mayor Robert Wagner of New York, a Catholic and a big-city Democrat. The third was Arthur Schlesinger, Jr., a spokesman for the liberal intellectuals in the Democratic party.

Their reaction to Mr. Johnson's speech was obvious. They approved. That meant the President's drive for consensus and continuity was doing very well. Now Mr. Johnson could turn to the budget.

Within twenty-four hours of the assassin's shot in Dallas, the President had a memo from Kermit Gordon, director of the Bureau of the Budget. The memo noted, "Despite the fact that the time is late, I know that you will want to make this budget your budget." By 6:00 on Sunday, the President was meeting with Gordon. By Tuesday morning, the day after Kennedy's burial, Mr. Johnson was at work on the budget, a task that continued for an hour or more daily for a month.

The outcome was a strategic victory. Instead of a $9 billion deficit, which the Kennedy budget had projected, Mr. Johnson's budget of $97.9 billion called for only a $4 billion deficit. This reduction would mean a lot to conservative, money-conscious congressmen when Congress took up the tax-cut bill, which Johnson wanted to stimulate the economy.

But more importantly, in moving swiftly to make the new budget his own, the President gave the U.S. government a new design, a new direction. He took money away from the Department of Defense and the Atomic Energy Commission and gave it to "human" areas like health care and medical research, education, housing, and anti-poverty programs. This was to be a theme of Mr. Johnson's Presidency. Later on, he would call it The Great Society.

If the President tried to lend a sense of urgency to the whole matter of tax cuts and budgets and White House-Capitol Hill relations in general, it was justified. At the moment, the stubborn Congress had no less than fifty pieces of proposed key legislation trapped in its committees and processes.

Other than the tax cut, the President was most concerned about the Civil Rights Act. This bill, more than anything else, could prove once and for all that he had escaped the South, that he was no longer troubled by how the voters back in Texas would respond.

Following the assassination, Mr. Johnson had moved quickly to reassure civil rights leaders. Just because the new President was a southerner, it didn't mean that the Kennedy Civil Rights Bill would be gutted. The compromises of 1957 were a thing of the past.

Much had changed since then. There had been ugly race riots in Birmingham, Alabama, in May, 1963, and the nation's racial scene remained troubled. Moreover, he was now President, not a Texas senator as in 1957. So between November 29 and December 5, Mr. Johnson talked personally with the major black leaders: Roy Wilkins, Whitney Young, Martin Luther King, James Farmer, Clarence Mitchell, and A.

Philip Randolph. He told them there would be no compromises. None at all.

The President went to unusual lengths to be helpful to Young, national director of the Urban League. In talking by phone with Young on Sunday, November 24, he learned that the urbane young black leader had not received an invitation to the Kennedy funeral. Mr. Johnson said Young should plan to come anyway.

Twenty minutes later, Young's telephone rang again. He expected to find Bill Moyers, Mr. Johnson's aide, or a secretary on the line, explaining that his invitation to the funeral had been cleared. But it was the President.

"I checked into that matter," he reassured the surprised Young. "There has been a slip-up. You come down tomorrow. There is a plane they tell me you really ought to take. It will get you in at 10:20 and you will be met by a White House car and the chauffeur will have your invitation." Just as the President said, a White House limousine met Young the next day and carried him to St. Matthew's Church for the Kennedy service.

The Civil Rights Bill equaled the highest hopes of Young and the other black leaders. For the first time, federal legislation authorized a mandatory Fair Employment Practices law, and it authorized the federal government to intervene in civil rights cases. By February 10, it had passed the House, 290 to 130.

In the Senate, as expected, the bill ran into a southern filibuster. But again, Mr. Johnson refused to compromise. After fifty-seven days, the longest filibuster in U.S. Senate history, the President's supporters forced a vote to end the speechmaking, and they won, 71 to 29. The Civil Rights Bill was signed into law by Mr. Johnson on July 2, and a piece of landmark legislation it was.

The personal lengths to which the President was interjecting himself into the legislative process were compared to Franklin Roosevelt's. The results were equally impressive. To beat back a threat to limit the President's authority in foreign affairs, Mr. Johnson daringly called the House of Representatives into session on, of all times, Christmas Eve. Many congressmen screamed, but Johnson won the vote he wanted. That was the first big test.

Within ten months, a flood of priority legislation had passed the Congress and been signed into law. This included the passage of the Tax Bill, the Civil Rights Bill, the Housing Act, the Food Stamp Bill, the War on Poverty, the Fire Island National Seashore Act, the Nurse Training Act, and the Urban Mass Transit Act. If anything, the legislative successes bolstered the feeling that, in the wake of John Kennedy's murder, the nation had achieved a mood and a pattern of continuity. And the breaking of the legislative logjam gave Mr. Johnson an excellent start on his 1964 campaign for a "mandate" of his own.

Presidents, like all politicians, have their personal as well as their public sides. And Mr. Johnson, being a spontaneous kind of man, had trouble keeping the two separated.

Come Eastertime in 1964, the President was back home in Texas. One summerlike afternoon during his stay, he invited four reporters to take a drive with him in his cream-colored Lincoln Continental. Before they realized it, the President was speeding along at ninety miles an hour. When one of the reporters gasped, Mr. Johnson quickly covered the speedometer with his five-gallon hat.

On Easter Sunday, the President astounded a carload of photographers who had been left behind by the Presidential car. It was headed toward Fredericksburg, where the Johnsons planned to attend church services. This time, the speed of the President's car was disputed by his press aides. But the photographers claimed they had driven eighty-five miles an hour seeking to catch up.

All of this—and more—was reported in the April 10, 1964, issue of *Time* magazine. The story angered Mr. Johnson terribly. He knew that there would be a strong public reaction to this kind of recklessness by a President of the United States, and he was right.

It came at a bad time. The calm that followed John Kennedy's assassination had been fading since the end of January. International tensions had picked up, with rioting in Panama, another Berlin incident, and new unrest in South Vietnam. In New York City, a huge racially motivated school boycott was brewing, and elsewhere racial tensions were strong. In addition, the Republican party was anxious to get back to politics. The GOP held a series of "Go-Day" dinners on January 29, and it looked as though they just might have an issue to go with—the Bobby Baker affair.

This embarrassment to the President involved Baker, the former Senate secretary and Mr. Johnson's protégé. It also involved a Maryland insurance man, Don B. Reynolds, a friend of Baker's. The story had actually hit the newspapers back in October, 1963, when the Washington *Post* said Baker was resigning his Senate job. Suspicion mounted that Baker had used his government position illegally to amass a personal fortune.

The afternoon that John Kennedy was shot, insuranceman Reynolds was testifying before the Senate Rules Committee.

In a closed session he told the senators about a business deal with Vice-President Johnson. Reynolds said one of Johnson's aides had pressured him into providing kickbacks in return for purchasing $200,000 in insurance on Johnson's life.

After the assassination, the press had let the issue lie, but now reporters were asking questions. Mr. Johnson counterattacked vigorously. He said a $542 stereo set he received from "the Baker family" was just a gift, and that in the other disputed matters, he saw no conflict of interest. That seemed to satisfy the press. The same day that news of Reynolds' testimony broke, Mr. Johnson ordered that unneeded lights at the White House be turned out. The publicity over the darkened White House got far more attention than the Bobby Baker affair. Now they were calling him "Lightbulb Lyndon."

One other minor flap happened before April ended. While showing some visitors the White House flower garden, Mr. Johnson picked up his pet beagle dogs, Him and Her, by the ears. When reporters told how much the dogs yelped, the nation's dog lovers yelped, too. This time, the President ignored the issue, staying busy at other things.

One reporter, James Reston of *The New York Times*, kept a log of the President's activities for the last seven days of April. Mr. Johnson held two formal and two informal press conferences. He made seven impromptu statements after White House meetings. He delivered a major foreign policy address to the Associated Press and helped settle the national railroad dispute. He opened the New York World's Fair and he talked at a political rally in Chicago. He was, frankly, setting the stage for the Democratic National Convention starting August 24 in Atlantic City, New Jersey.

It was hot in Washington, D.C., almost ninety degrees, but the President wasn't worried. Just two days earlier, a team of physicians had signed a report saying his health was normal. Eyes, lungs, abdomen, blood, heart, everything. So, shortly after lunch, Mr. Johnson decided to take a walk around the south lawn drive of the White House. As he often did, he invited the White House press corps to tag along on this Wednesday, August 26.

The birds were chirping in the trees. Gardeners were busy tending the White House lawns, and the President's dogs were happily tumbling along, a scene that was far different from the one at Atlantic City. There, 140 miles away, the scene was chaotic. There were 5,260 delegates in town, at least that many newspeople and perhaps twice that many hangers-on. Staffs at the resort city's hotels, used to fun-seeking conventioneers, were near collapse from the pressures. And yet, the most frenzied part of the Democratic convention was still to come. The nominations would occur that night.

That was what the reporters with Johnson wanted him to talk about. Who would be his Vice-Presidential running mate?

He was still considering that problem, the President insisted with a straight face. He had, in fact, been on the telephone much of the morning, asking his political friends what he should do. But, he claimed, he had reached no decision.

What about Hubert Humphrey?

"I've asked Senator Humphrey to come down this afternoon and talk just so I can get his ideas on the Vice-Presidency," Mr. Johnson said vaguely. "That is, if he can work it into his schedule. If he can come down, I'll let you know."

As early as July 29, the President had shrewdly eliminated ambitious Robert Kennedy, the Attorney General, as a possible running mate. He had simply announced that no members of his Cabinet would be considered. Thereafter, most political observers believed that his choice would be Hubert Humphrey. Humphrey believed it, too.

The President, enjoying all of the suspense, let it be known that he was also considering Senator Eugene McCarthy of Minnesota. On Saturday, August 22, Mr. Johnson had added to key aides that he might switch at the last minute to Senate Majority Leader Mike Mansfield.

But at the White House on this sunny afternoon, Mr. Johnson was nearing the end of his cat-and-mouse games. The reporters sensed that his mood was buoyant, teasing, expansive. They suspected he had already made up his mind.

By now some of the women reporters had dropped out, seeking a shade tree to sit under. It looked as though Mr. Johnson was going for a new record, surpassing the nine laps around the White House lawn that he had hiked the previous Monday.

What about the campaign?

The only campaigning he was going to do was right over there in the Oval Office, he replied. Doing his job.

What about Senator Barry Goldwater, the Republican nominee?

The Republican nominee was frightening everyone with all his talk about "extremism in the defense of liberty . . ."

What about a possible backlash from white voters angry at the recent Negro rioting in New York City, Rochester, Paterson, Elizabeth, Chicago, and Philadelphia?

"Backlash" was simply a pet word among reporters and

political writers, Mr. Johnson insisted. He was more interested in the "frontlash"—the reaction to Goldwater's radical politics.

What about the emotional clash at Atlantic City earlier that week? The one between the white regular Mississippi delegation and the black Mississippi Freedom Party delegation, both of which wanted to be seated?

"The Democratic party has been the House of Protest since it was born," the President retorted.

Fifteen times that afternoon, the President trooped around the south lawn drive, a total of 4.35 miles. Finally, about 3:00, he headed up to the Oval Office for an orange drink. Later that night, on board an airplane headed for Atlantic City, he sipped Sanka as he watched a TV set showing John Connally of Texas nominating him for President. With Mr. Johnson on the plane was his Vice-Presidential choice, Hubert Humphrey.

For three months, the Johnson-Humphrey and Goldwater-William E. Miller teams campaigned for the Presidency of the United States.

It was no contest. Goldwater's shoot-from-the-hip comments scared a lot of staid Republican businessmen. The Democratic-controlled economy was booming for the fourth straight year. The murder of the young President in Dallas was also a factor—hard to measure, but always there. It aided the Democrats.

On election night, there was never any doubt.

Mr. Johnson won 61 per cent of the popular vote, a total of 43,126,757. He won 486 electoral votes, the highest since Roosevelt's 1936 victory. He won 90 per cent of the black vote, and he carried every congressional district in thirty-two states outside of the South.

But of most importance to him, he won his own term, to be endowed with his own design. "It seems to me tonight," he said in Austin on election eve, "that I have spent my whole life getting ready for this moment."

Chapter 12

MANDATE

President Johnson was inaugurated on a wintry Wednesday. After taking the oath of office, he talked to the crowds about how important it was to keep the country moving. He spoke of "the excitement of becoming—always becoming, trying, probing, falling, resting, and trying again—but always trying and always gaining."

After that, the 375 members of the Mormon Tabernacle Choir sang, and the U.S. Marine Band played. There was a luncheon in the old Supreme Court Chamber, and that afternoon, the President was driven down Pennsylvania Avenue to the White House. From a reviewing stand, he and Lady Bird watched the Inaugural Parade, which lasted two and a half hours. For a time, Mr. Johnson had his beagle, Him, at his side.

There were five Inaugural balls. At each, starting at the Mayflower Hotel, the President and Mrs. Johnson stayed a few minutes, dancing and greeting friends and supporters. They especially enjoyed the last stop, at the Sheraton Park Hotel. Many of their Texas friends were there, celebrating. Mr.

Johnson, in high spirits, told them, "Never have so many paid so much to dance so little." It was near midnight when the Johnsons returned home.

The next evening, the President developed a rending cough. He also complained of chest pains. The whispered concern of his staff was that he was having another heart attack, but at Bethesda Naval Hospital doctors said it was only a cold. They prescribed bed rest, and it was not until the following Tuesday, January 26, that the President returned home, still weakened and bedfast, to the White House.

The 1600 Pennsylvania Avenue home of the U.S. Presidents has changed a great deal since June, 1800, when John Adams moved the U.S. capital from urbane Philadelphia to frontier Washington. That year, the White House was unfinished. But no matter. Even when the workmen finally left in 1803, Abigail Adams, the President's wife, disliked the white, brilliant, looming edifice with the grooved columns in front. To her, it was big and impersonal.

It is, today, even bigger.

In 1902 a west wing was added to the main building, an ambitious project promoted by Theodore Roosevelt. Soon after, an east wing was built, adding more offices. After a hundred years, this country finally had a huge, elegant home for its Chief Executive, one that had 131 rooms and covered eighteen acres. It ran, as any map of Washington shows, all the way from East Executive Avenue across to West Executive.

While living there, many Presidents and their families have left their mark. Franklin Roosevelt put in a swimming pool; Harry Truman, three bowling alleys. Dwight Eisenhower had a putting green set up. When it came John Kennedy's turn, except for a rocking chair, he left the alterations mostly to his wife, Jackie. It was her idea to restore the inside of the White House, allowing a full measure of its elegance and historical importance. Through the years, many valuable White House items—furniture, dinnerware, paintings, rugs—had been sold, and she called for their return. The response of the public was good, and the restoration project was virtually finished when Mr. Kennedy was killed.

One touch that Lyndon Johnson brought immediately to the White House was a highly practical one. Beneath a portrait of George Washington, Mr. Johnson had three television sets and two news tickers installed in the Oval Office. Not that any President ever lacks for news. In the two-level Situation Room below, there were news tickers for the Associated Press, United Press International, Reuters, the FBI Service, and the Foreign Broadcast Service, and the President was immediately informed of important reports. But President Johnson took a highly personal interest in the news, especially the news about himself.

The Oval Office is only roughly oval, since two inside walls meet at a right angle. It measures perhaps fifty feet by forty. For his Presidential desk, Mr. Johnson chose the same sturdy mahogany model with the gray-green leather top that he had used for years in the Senate. In front of the desk were two sofas and a marble-topped coffee table. A drawer slid out of the coffee table with a telephone and buttons to forty-two separate lines. Like Mr. Kennedy, Mr. Johnson also had a rocker.

Rather than the Oval Office, it was to the Fish Room that the President had summoned his legislative lobbyists early in January, 1965, for an old-fashioned pep rally. The victory that Mr. Johnson had in mind was essentially a victory over the Eighty-ninth Congress, which in the next few months would be deciding the fate of the President's proposed Great Society programs.

"I have watched the Congress from either the inside or the outside, man and boy, for more than forty years," the President told his assistants, "and I've never seen a Congress that didn't eventually take the measure of the President it was dealing with."

He meant, in other words, that there was little time to lose. Right now, Mr. Johnson admitted, he was strong. His overwhelming victory over Senator Goldwater had, in a way, given him a mandate from the people. The Democrats, moreover, had retained a 2-to-1 majority in the Senate and gained a 295-to-140 edge in the House. That spelled "power," but Mr. Johnson knew that it wouldn't last.

The President had a goal: He wanted Congress to pass more legislation during his First Hundred Days, which ended April 13, than it had during FDR's First Hundred. And Congress did.

The bills to establish a professional photography week, a Goddard Day in honor of the famed rocket scientist, and Nez Perce National Park in Idaho were relatively unimportant. But with only four of Mr. Johnson's First Hundred Days remaining, the Senate passed a federal school aid bill, completing what had been a Democratic goal for years and years. Another long-time Democratic aim, medical care for the aged, was within reach. It passed the House before Easter, and the Senate would pass Medicare in July.

On vote after vote, the stolid Democratic majority rubber-stamped the Administration's 1965 legislative proposals: aid to Appalachia, a liberalization of immigration laws, a new Cabinet department, a major housing bill, and a voting rights law.

By April 8, Mr. Johnson could rightfully claim that his Hundred Days made "a record of major accomplishments without equal or close parallel in the present era." By October, when Congress recessed, 90 of the Administration's 115 legislative recommendations had been passed by Congress and signed into law. *Newsweek* magazine called him "Lyndon the Powerful . . . He summons the dukes and barons of Congress to his chambers and they dutifully carry out his royal decrees."

But that kind of talk, which the President unfortunately encouraged, could only spell trouble. "There were a lot of us who broke our backs on some of these bills," grumbled one senator, "but Lyndon claimed he did it all himself. And you don't make friends that way." What Mr. Johnson was doing, one lobbyist observed, was "stockpiling adversity."

It was a serious mistake, a reality that became clearer and clearer during the second session of the Eighty-ninth Congress. By then, President Johnson had already experienced several crises, one of which—perhaps the gravest—started in a little town in Alabama named Selma.

The briefing for the congressmen had run long, and the President was tired. But when a Presidential aide quietly placed a folded note in Mr. Johnson's hands, the fatigue was quickly forgotten. Frowning into his glasses, the President read that the Rev. James Reeb had just died.

The message was sad, and ominous. Reeb, a thirty-eight-year-old Bostonian, had traveled to Selma to march with Dr. Martin Luther King's protesters. Two days before—on March 7—he had been severely beaten by four white Selma residents who accused him of being a "nigger-lover." The death of the white Unitarian minister was certain to darken the nation's ugly racial picture.

Mr. Johnson and Lady Bird excused themselves from the reception for the congressmen and their wives. They felt a responsibility to Mrs. Reeb and planned to call her at once, expressing their sympathy.

Outside the White House gates, the Johnsons could hear civil rights demonstrators marching, singing, shouting. They carried placards, each one bearing a message for the President. One read, "LBJ, just you wait. . . . See what happens in '68."

The 1968 campaign could—and would—wait. The President was preoccupied with what was going to happen that night, the next day, and the next.

The Rev. Dr. King, a skilled strategist, was pressing his nonviolent voting rights campaign relentlessly. For a battleground, he had chosen Selma, a town of 15,100 blacks and 14,440 whites. That was Selma's population; the names on the voting rolls, however, were 99 per cent white. It was clearly a miscarriage of American constitutional intent, but what could and should be done about it?

Personally, the President had no sympathy for demonstrations or for demonstrators. In his opinion, the important battles for civil rights would be won in the halls of Congress, not in the streets of Alabama. But it was a political problem he could not ignore. The civil rights factions wanted him to send federal troops to Alabama to protect Dr. King's marchers, who were being beaten, clubbed, jailed, spit on, and verbally abused. If the President refused, he would be accused of being a racist. If he acted too quickly, he would make a states' rights martyr of Governor George Wallace, Alabama's staunch segregationist. The President wanted neither development.

On Friday, to Mr. Johnson's surprise, the Alabama governor sent a telegram asking for a special meeting to discuss Selma.

The President and the governor met in the Oval Office the following day at noon. Eyeing Wallace coolly, Mr. Johnson got the impression, as he later wrote, that the governor was "a nervous, aggressive man; a rough, shrewd politician who had managed to touch the deepest chords of pride as well as prejudice among his people." During their somewhat strained talks, Governor Wallace agreed to use state troops to protect the marchers who planned to walk from Selma to Montgomery on March 25. Mr. Johnson nodded, agreeing that this was the best way. But it was not a promise that the governor kept.

While the President pondered the question of using federal troops, the Justice Department was finishing up a speedily written forty-eight-page draft of a new voting rights bill. By Sunday morning, March 14, the draft was in the President's hands. Mr. Johnson wanted to deliver the bill to the Congress personally, a move that had its risks. As a very minimum, the President knew that he needed the approval of congressional leaders.

In a five o'clock meeting that Sunday afternoon, Senator Mike Mansfield spoke first—and he argued against a personal appearance by the President. Mansfield had played an important role in getting the 1964 Civil Rights Bill passed, and he would again have a major part in guiding any 1965 bill through the Senate.

Senator Everett Dirksen of Illinois agreed, fearing that Mr. Johnson's appearance would be taken as a sign of panic. "This is a deliberate government," the senator said in his raspy voice. "Don't let these people say we scared him into it. Don't circumvent the Congress."

Next to voice an opinion was Speaker John McCormack of Massachusetts, sitting there with his white hair combed straight back. "I disagree," the Speaker said. "I strongly recommend that the President go to the Congress and present the bill to a joint session. Such a speech would show bipartisanship. It would show the world that action is being taken."

At that point, the tide of opinion shifted. Majority Leader Carl Albert said he liked McCormack's idea. He told the President, "I don't think your coming before Congress would be a sign of panic. I think it would help." With the others present—Senator Thomas Kuchel of California and Reps. Hale Boggs of Louisiana and William McCulloch of Ohio—agreeing that the President should visit the Congress, it was decided. Mr. Johnson would speak at 9 P.M. the next day. This would be the first time since 1946 that a special message to Congress had been delivered personally by a President. That year, Harry Truman had unsuccessfully asked for powers to break a nation-wide railroad strike.

That night, the President's writers typed from midnight until dawn, seeking to expand Mr. Johnson's general outline into a powerful, morally persuasive speech. At 6 P.M. the next day, the speech was still being brought to Mr. Johnson, a page at a time. An hour later, he was still editing it line by line. At 8 P.M., less than an hour before he was to give the speech, he was still at work on an ending.

"Let's close it up the way we closed the one where I talked about growing up in the Hill Country," he told his aide, Jack Valenti. "Let's talk about teaching the Mexicans in Cotulla, the first job I had after I left college." He had learned plenty about poverty and prejudice on that job.

Shortly after nine, the trumpet-like voice of William M. "Fishbait" Miller, the House doorkeeper, carried out of the packed House chamber: "The President of the United States."

The lights were blinding in Mr. Johnson's eyes, and he could barely see Lady Bird and daughter Lynda in the Presidential box. On the chamber floor, he caught glimpses of the faces of some of the southern congressmen, and the President knew they were against him.

But he began. "I speak tonight for the dignity of man and the destiny of democracy," Mr. Johnson said, his face a picture of great concern. "At times history and fate meet at a single time in a single place to shape a turning point in man's unending search for freedom. So it was at Lexington and Concord. So it was a century ago at Appomattox. So it was last week in Selma, Alabama."

After that opening, the phrases came faster, although it was an unusually long speech that lay open before the President. . . .

"There is no constitutional issue here. . . . There is no moral issue. . . . There is no issue of states' rights or national rights. There is only the struggle for human rights. . . .

"What happened in Selma is part of a far larger movement which reaches into every section and state of America. . . .

"Their cause must be our cause, too. . . .

"And . . . we . . . shall . . . overcome."

Counting the automatic responses at the beginning and the end, the Congress gave Mr. Johnson four standing ovations in the space of forty-two minutes. The tumbling applause, which came in waves, was a welcome sign.

On March 18, when Governor Wallace told him that Alabama could not protect Dr. King's marchers, the President federalized the Alabama National Guard. With the aid of regular soldiers and federal marshals, they would guard the civil rights marchers.

By August, the Congress had acted. Both houses had risen

to the challenge, passing a civil rights bill that no one had really believed would be brought up that year, much less passed into law. On August 6, the President returned to the Capitol to sign the Voting Rights Act of 1965. Before a statue of Abraham Lincoln, in the rotunda of the Capitol, Mr. Johnson observed that the nation was moving "step by step—often painfully, but I think with clear vision—along the path toward American freedom." The racial conflicts in America were far from ended, but at that event on that particular day, the Presidency of Lyndon B. Johnson very probably reached its highest point.

Then Mr. Johnson began to lose his grip on his 1964 election mandate. Even as he rushed swiftly to his goal with his civil rights legislation, the President was stumbling, a little bit at a time.

It was a crisis born of power. Too much power, in some ways. A misunderstanding of power, in others.

The crisis was not born exclusively with Mr. Johnson and his Presidency. It began, in a very real sense, with the 1787 Constitution. It began with the reluctance of the Founding Fathers to limit greatly the powers of the Presidency. And so, President after President after President, these powers had grown. And yet, there are *some* limits to a President's power. Says historian Emmet John Hughes, "The President—*any* President—has some power to do almost anything, absolute power to do a few things, but never full power to do all things."

It was Mr. Johnson's confusion over what he could and could not do with his power that began to weaken his Presidency.

According to Professor Alfred De Grazia, one of the

powers of the President is "to create crisis." Mr. Johnson understood this technique well. He used it, for example, to justify the landing of U.S. Marines in the Dominican Republic in late April, 1965. But not everyone believed that this crisis was real. In the aftermath, the President found that he had lost the liberal members of his Great Society consensus, and so he no longer had a consensus. That made the Dominican affair a costly crisis, real or not.

The revolt in the Dominican Republic was between supporters of a former President, Juan Bosch, and supporters of a group of right-wing generals. The Bosch supporters were called the Rebels and the generals' supporters, Loyalists. President Johnson believed—rightly or wrongly—that the Rebels were mostly Communists. Fearing "another Cuba," where the Communists had gained control, the President chose to back the Loyalists.

On the afternoon of April 28, it looked as though the Loyalists might be losing. That was when U.S. Ambassador W. Tapley Bennett cabled Washington for the help of the U.S. Marines. They were waiting offshore, on the aircraft carrier *Boxer*. The order to land came from President Johnson at 6:30 P.M.

Realizing the seriousness of "invading" a foreign country, the President acted swiftly to get the approval of both Congress and the Organization of American States, a "United Nations" of South American countries.

But the OAS dragged its feet. Some congressmen were asking hard questions and such big guns of the press as *The New York Times*, the Washington *Post* and columnist Walter Lippmann were on the warpath. *The Times* charged the President with showing "little awareness . . . that the Dominican people—not just a handful of Communists—were fighting and dying for social justice and constitutionalism."

In defense, Mr. Johnson claimed that the American Embassy had been under attack. At one point, he told newsmen, "Some fifteen hundred innocent people were murdered and shot, and their heads cut off," and that "our ambassador . . . had a thousand American men, women, and children assembled in [a] hotel who were pleading with their President to help preserve their lives."

But when Ambassador Bennett testified before the Senate Foreign Relations Committee, he admitted that none of this was true.

For weeks, Mr. Johnson issued statements daily on the Dominican crisis. And each time, his credibility gap seemed to grow.

By September, Senator J. William Fulbright of Arkansas could remain quiet no longer. In a Senate speech, he charged that Mr. Johnson's decision to land the Marines had been based on inadequate information or, in some cases, simply false information. Fulbright was the chairman of the Senate Foreign Relations Committee, and he denounced any broad policy of intervention in the affairs of other countries. Up to now, he had supported Mr. Johnson, while often disagreeing.

Now, Senator Fulbright was breaking with the Johnson administration in a highly critical way, and he was taking most of the congressional liberals with him. It didn't matter that, in June, 1966, Juan Bosch was defeated in an election by a moderate right-wing candidate, Joaquin Balaguer, and stability returned to the little Caribbean country. For Mr. Johnson, the damage was already done. And the setbacks for the President were just beginning.

On October 8, after weeks of pain, the President underwent an operation. His gallbladder was removed, plus a kidney stone. When he left Bethesda Naval Hospital, he went home to the LBJ Ranch. For twelve weeks, he convalesced, working on his budget and his 1966 State of the Union address. But even that speech was to create problems for him.

The speech was too long, but that was more a symptom than a cause of Mr. Johnson's coming difficulties. The speech was too long because it spoke of too many legislative requests. After the landslide of bills passed in 1965, lawmakers expected the second session of the Eighty-ninth Congress to be much more leisurely. Instead, the President was proposing one new bill after another.

With a war going on in Southeast Asia, the Congress expected fewer Great Society programs. Instead, Mr. Johnson was saying, "I believe we can continue the Great Society while we fight in Vietnam." A short time later, he proposed a record $112.8 billion budget, which reinforced his commitment to both guns and butter.

Again, Mr. Johnson had misjudged the powers of the Presidency. Buoyed by his legislative triumphs in 1964 and 1965, he had assumed that he could pressure Congress into reacting the same way in 1966. But Congress was ready to revolt. Judging from its mood, Mr. Johnson had asked for more than he was going to get.

That was the case, as it turned out. By the following January, when he delivered his 1967 State of the Union message, Mr. Johnson talked no longer of both guns and butter. His administration, he said, would "do all we can with what we have, knowing that it is far, far more than we have ever done before, and far, far less than our problems will ultimately require." There was much less talk of the Great

Society in that speech, and more talk of war, the war in Vietnam.

Within a few months, the White House Situation Room was concerned with far more than just the fighting in Southeast Asia. On June 5, at 4:35 A.M., Mr. Johnson was awakened and told that war had broken out between Israel and the Arabs in the Middle East. Three hours later, the President was told that "the hot line is up." For the first time, the Soviet Union was calling on the special teletype circuit linking Washington and Moscow. The message was about the Middle East war, and it was an ominous message. The Russians were threatening to interfere.

For several days, the Soviet Union rattled its sabers. And the United States rattled its right back.

A ceasefire was finally arranged on June 10. A few days later, Mr. Johnson held a summit meeting in this country with Soviet Premier Aleksei Kosygin. They talked for more than five hours at Glassboro State College in New Jersey. "I left Glassboro on Sunday evening, June 25, with mixed feelings— disappointment that we had not solved any major problems but hopeful that we had moved to a better understanding of our differences," Mr. Johnson wrote in *The Vantage Point.*

In July, the shooting drew much closer to the White House than the Middle East. First in Newark and a few days later in Detroit, major race riots occurred. Detroit was the hardest hit—27 dead, 800 injured, 2,455 arrested and $200 million in property damages. At one point, just before Mr. Johnson authorized the use of federal troops in Detroit, J. Edgar Hoover, the FBI director, reported, "They have lost all control in Detroit. Harlem may break loose within thirty minutes. They plan to tear it to pieces."

But these problems, real as they were, were not Mr.

Johnson's major problem. An unruly Congress, a war in the Middle East, riots in Newark and Detroit—none of these would destroy his administration's effectiveness to govern. But there was another factor that very well could do that, another war. It was the war in Vietnam, *that* war, the one that just wouldn't go away. The war in Vietnam was, increasingly, at the core of Mr. Johnson's troubles.

By the time the President came to the Capitol to deliver his 1968 State of the Union address, most congressmen and many Americans had forgotten Mr. Johnson's triumphs in behalf of the country. They had forgotten how he welded the nation together following John Kennedy's death. How he pushed a flood of much-needed legislation through a balky Congress. How he had directed an era of economic prosperity.

Thirty-four of the nation's one hundred U.S. senators didn't even attend Mr. Johnson's State of the Union speech on January 17, 1968. That's how bitter feelings had become in the Congress about a monstrous U.S. land war in a tiny Southeast Asian country. It was there, in the Vietnam jungles, that the real powers of Lyndon Johnson's Presidency wasted away.

Chapter 13

VIETNAM

Within forty-eight hours after John Kennedy's death, Mr. Johnson was meeting with key aides and advisers on the matter of Vietnam. Little did he know, or even suspect, that this tiny Asian country, so far from Washington, would soon dominate and weaken his Presidency.

The new President, in taking over from John Kennedy, viewed the situation in Vietnam in much the same way that Mr. Kennedy had viewed it. And Mr. Kennedy's views—in their essentials—had been very similar to President Dwight Eisenhower's views. That is how long the Vietnam Question had plagued U.S. foreign policy makers.

Before the United States became deeper and deeper involved in Vietnam's ill-fated fortunes, it had been the French who had tried to shape the little country's destiny. For eight years, the French had fought there unsuccessfully, losing tens of thousands of men and billions of dollars. The turning point came in 1954, at a French base called Dien Bien Phu. The French lost that battle resoundingly.

Mr. Eisenhower had been President in 1954, the year that

the Geneva Conference on Indochina finally brought an end to eight years of bloody fighting. The French had been battling Communist forces that called themselves the Vietminh. They were led by a near-legendary figure named Ho Chi Minh. Mr. Johnson had never met Ho, but during the next five years, the new President would probably spend more time thinking about Ho Chi Minh than he would about any other man on earth. For the United States, or so many of its critics would later claim, was about to repeat most of the mistakes of the French.

To the surprise of many, Ho Chi Minh agreed under the 1954 Geneva accords to withdraw his forces north of the 17th Parallel. That left South Vietnam in the hands of Emperor Bao Dai, but since the emperor spent most of his time in Europe, he was quickly supplanted by his hand-picked premier, Ngo Dinh Diem.

Under the terms of the Geneva agreements, an all-Vietnam "national" election was scheduled for July, 1956, and that was probably the reason that Ho Chi Minh had agreed to withdraw. He expected to win, thus controlling all of Vietnam. And if the election had been held, most observers believed he would have won. But Premier Diem, fearful of Ho's popularity, refused to allow any balloting in the South, and so the two countries remained divided.

President Eisenhower, fearing a Communist takeover of all of Southeast Asia, signed on as a supporter of the Diem government. In view of the recent French military losses, Mr. Eisenhower elected not to involve U.S. troops. But in a letter dated October 23, 1954, the American President did offer U.S. economic aid to South Vietnam. The only proviso was that Premier Diem reform his government. It showed strong signs of becoming a dictatorship.

The reforms never came, a reality that President Eisenhower chose to ignore. Within three years, Diem's enemies were trying to assassinate him.

The causes of their anger were many—Diem's ouster of thousands of village chiefs, his obvious bias against Vietnam's millions of Buddhists (he was a Catholic), the plentiful acts of terror by his chief advisers, who included three of his brothers and his much-feared wife, Madame Nhu. But a murder attempt in February, 1957, failed, and so did an attempted *coup* by some of Vietnam's crack paratroopers on November 11, 1960.

With the opposition to the ruling regime growing, a group of the country's anti-Diem leaders met in December, 1960, and organized the National Liberation Front of South Vietnam (the NLF). In a matter of a few weeks, the NLF was busily pursuing its goal: guerilla warfare against Diem's 250,000-man army. Nine days after John Kennedy's inauguration, the Ho Chi Minh government in Hanoi, the North Vietnamese capital, announced its support of the NLF, making more ominous the guerillas' terrorist tactics.

But rather than Vietnam, it was the tiny Southeast Asian country of Laos that commanded Mr. Kennedy's attention early in his term. Working from two northern provinces, the Communists were turning the country into a base from which to strike at other countries, including South Vietnam. President Kennedy placed nearby U.S. troops on alert, and this "saber-rattling" convinced the Communist forces to join in a shaky ceasefire. In July, 1962, a neutrality pact for Laos was signed in Geneva.

By this time, the United States was already involved militarily in Vietnam. A letter from President Kennedy carried personally to Ngo Dinh Diem in May, 1961, by Vice-President

Johnson had made clear the U.S.'s growing concern about the Communist activities there. ". . . We are prepared to initiate in collaboration with your government a series of joint, mutually-supporting actions in the military, political, economic and other fields," wrote Mr. Kennedy. By mid-1962, the number of American military advisers in Vietnam had been increased from the 700 originally dispatched in 1961 to about 11,000.

Why had Mr. Kennedy so quickly escalated the U.S. involvement in Vietnam? Certainly, the Diem regime's plight was precarious. But there were some observers who suggested that Mr. Kennedy's decision resulted from other troubles. One was the embarrassing Bay of Pigs incident, in which Cuba's Communist leader Fidel Castro easily repelled a mini-invasion of Cuban exiles trained by the U.S. Central Intelligence Agency. Three months later in Vienna, Mr. Kennedy was upbraided by Soviet dictator Nikita Khrushchev, who thought the American President was weak and could be bullied. So in taking a strong stand in Vietnam, Mr. Kennedy may have been deeply concerned about his image.

By late 1963, Mr. Kennedy had dispatched about 16,000 U.S. troops to Vietnam. The President emphasized, however, "We can give them equipment, we can send our men out there as advisers, but they have to win it, the people of Vietnam, against the Communists." Mr. Kennedy also added that the Diem government was "out of touch with the people," and he was tragically right. Just three weeks before Kennedy himself was shot and killed, Ngo Dinh Diem was assassinated.

This, then, was the discouraging state of affairs that confronted Lyndon Johnson as he assumed the Presidency. Within a month, he was being briefed by Defense Secretary Robert McNamara, who had just returned from Vietnam. "The situation is very disturbing," McNamara said. "Current trends, unless reversed in the next two or three months, will lead to neutralization at best and more likely to a Communist-controlled state."

That was why the new President's first major decision on Vietnam had been to reaffirm President Kennedy's policies. And that was also why, in August, 1964, his second major decision was to order retaliation for the much-discussed Tonkin Gulf incident and then to ask Congress for a blank-check resolution in support of his Southeast Asia policies.

Congress quickly complied. But then, later, a lot of congressmen began to have second thoughts. . . .

The USS *Maddox*, an American destroyer, was attacked off the coast of North Vietnam on August 2, 1964, by three North Vietnamese torpedo boats—of that much information, everyone could agree on.

But later, there were many critics who would question whether the USS *Maddox* and its sister destroyer, the *C. Turner Joy*, were also attacked in the Gulf of Tonkin by enemy torpedo boats about 8 A.M. Washington time on August 4.

This "alleged" second attack prompted President Johnson to take two actions:

(1) Send American planes to bomb North Vietnam in a deliberate, major act of war, and

(2) Ask the Congress to approve a resolution to make "clear that our government is united in its determination to take all necessary measures in support of freedom, and in defense of peace, in Southeast Asia."

Writing in *The Vantage Point*, Mr. Johnson said, "I believe that President Truman's one mistake in courageously going to the defense of South Korea in 1950 had been his failure to ask Congress for an expression of its backing. He could have had it easily, and it would have strengthened his hand. I had made up my mind not to repeat that error . . ."

Within three days, on August 7, Mr. Johnson had his "Gulf of Tonkin Resolution." In the House, the vote had been unanimous, 416 to 0. Only two of the one hundred senators— Ernest Gruening of Alaska and Wayne Morse of Oregon— voted against the document.

Now Mr. Johnson had in his hands a congressional resolution authorizing him to "take all necessary measures to repel any armed attack against the forces of the United States and to prevent further aggression." In other words, the President held a blank check to go to war— or so Mr. Johnson believed at the time and so he intended.

Even some members of the President's own staff felt that the resolution was being acted on too hastily. At one staff briefing, Douglass Cater, a new White House adviser on domestic issues, questioned McGeorge Bundy. "Isn't this a little precipitous?" Cater asked. "Do we have all the information . . ."

Bundy responded sharply. "The President has decided and that's what we're doing."

Cater, still in doubt, replied, "Gee, Mac, I haven't really thought it through."

"Don't," Bundy said.

There were cogent reasons why Bundy didn't want too many questions asked. One was that the evidence was sketchy and inconclusive about whether the second Tonkin attack had ever occurred. But the problem was much broader: in the past several weeks, the Johnson administration had been concealing the nature of its naval activities off the North Vietnamese coast. Both the people and the Congress had been badly deceived. "That was the central issue, not whether or not there was a second Tonkin episode," wrote Pulitzer Prize-winning reporter David Halberstam in *The Best and the Brightest.*

Since January, under a cover of secrecy, U.S. Gen. Paul Harkins had been commanding a series of hit-and-run raids against North Vietnam. These raids were launched from Saigon, the South Vietnamese capital, the activities bearing the code name of 34A. The personnel were Vietnamese—the paratroopers, the frog men, and the crews of the torpedo boats staging the commando raids up and down the North Vietnamese coast. But the operations themselves were planned and directed by the U.S. Military Assistance Command, Vietnam— planned and directed by General Harkins and McGeorge Bundy. It was plainly an American-controlled operation.

So the fiction that the American destroyers, the *Maddox* and the *C. Turner Joy,* were just randomly singled out on the international high seas for an unprovoked attack was just that: fiction. In point of fact, as the *Maddox* had headed north on July 31, it had passed three South Vietnamese PT boats returning from a 34A mission. For all the North Vietnamese knew, the *Maddox* and the *C. Turner Joy* were part of the 34A operation. Intercepted radio messages showed that this was exactly what the enemy had concluded.

But Congress knew virtually nothing about the extent of American control over the 34A operations, and Defense Secretary McNamara wasn't about to give them the whole, truthful story. As a consequence, instead of full Senate hearings on Mr. Johnson's proposed resolution, there had been only a few, quickly answered questions.

The leaders of any effective full-scale congressional revolt would have had to have been Senator Fulbright and his Foreign Relations Committee. But, irony of ironies, it was

Senator Fulbright who was *managing* the Tonkin Gulf Resolution in the Senate. It wasn't that the senator from Arkansas had no questions about the expanding war and about the Johnson resolution. It was just that . . . well, he had been a close personal friend of Mr. Johnson's for a long time, and if there were any plans afoot to turn Vietnam into a large-scale conflict, Senator Fulbright believed that he would have a chance privately to argue against them.

So when Senator Gaylord Nelson of Wisconsin offered an amendment that would limit the American role in Vietnam, it was Fulbright himself who persuaded Nelson to withdraw it. That left only Senators Gruening and Morse against the resolution. Morse said, ". . . We are in effect giving the President . . . warmaking powers in the absence of a declaration of war. I believe that to be a historic mistake."

Down the road a few months, Senator Fulbright would agree. He would even take to the Senate floor to apologize profusely to Senator Nelson for misleading him. But in the late summer of 1964, with a Presidential election scheduled soon, the Tonkin Gulf Resolution looked like a resounding success for Mr. Johnson. Now he could escalate the Vietnam War at will.

He waited until after his election victory over Senator Barry Goldwater, and until after his inauguration on January 20, 1965. Then on Sunday, February 7, the President was handed an urgent message from Gen. William Westmoreland, the new U.S. commander in Saigon. The message said that the Viet Cong had struck at three Vietnam bases, with the worst damage at Pleiku, where 7 U.S. soldiers were dead and 109 injured. Now Mr. Johnson had the right incident at the right time to justify escalating the war.

That night, U.S. planes bombed Dong Hoi and Van Linh,

two North Vietnamese bases. Three days later, the Viet Cong guerillas struck again, and again U.S. planes flew out to bomb North Vietnam sites. There were more Viet Cong raids, and more U.S. bombing. And more fighting. By the end of 1965, there were 190,000 American troops in South Vietnam, and already 1,350 Americans had died and 5,300 had been injured.

"We are not going to send American boys nine or ten thousand miles away from home to do what Asian boys ought to be doing for themselves," Mr. Johnson had thundered while campaigning in October, 1964. But those words were hollow now. For the Vietnam War was now an American war. And a lot of those American boys, and more to come, would die.

As early as February, 1966, as many as thirty of the sixty-seven Democratic senators were against any further escalating of the Vietnam War. The list included such names as Fulbright, Kennedy, Morse, Mansfield, Hartke, McGovern, Young, Gruening, Gore, Church, Moss, Bartlett, Burdick, Aiken, and Clark. They were called, and called themselves, the Doves.

Senator Stephen Young of Ohio probably spoke for most Doves on the Vietnam issue when, on June 22, 1966, he told the President, "It's a miserable civil war. And it does not involve in any strategic importance the defense of the United States or any real commitment. We don't have a mandate from Almighty God to police the entire world. This talk about there being an international Communist conspiracy that we must repel wherever it rears its ugly head is a myth. Southeast Asia, Mr. President, very definitely is not within our sphere of influence."

The President and his chief advisers were, virtually to a man, deserving of the descriptive title of Hawks. McNamara (at least for a time), Bundy, Secretary of State Dean Rusk, Vice-President Humphrey, the Joint Chiefs of Staff—they were all Hawks. Perhaps the only exception was George Ball, the Undersecretary of State. Of all the close Johnson advisers on the war, only Ball, a New Deal lawyer from Chicago, warned early against escalating, against getting caught in a Vietnam quagmire. It wasn't that Ball opposed the use of military power. He just didn't like to see it wasted, and he viewed Vietnam as a bottomless swamp for American interests.

It was Ball who wrote in October, 1964, "Once on the tiger's back we cannot be sure of picking the place to dismount." But as a voice of moderation, a voice of reason, Ball's voice within the inner counsels of Lyndon Johnson's administration was a voice crying in the wilderness.

Ball was still arguing against a prolonged Asia land war against local guerillas in late July, 1965. But he lost the argument, and in his memoirs, Mr. Johnson explained why he disagreed with his undersecretary's position.

"First, from all the evidence available to me it seemed likely that all of Southeast Asia would pass under Communist control, slowly or quickly, but inevitably, at least down to Singapore but almost certainly to Djakarta. . . .

"Second, I knew our people well enough to realize that if we walked away from Vietnam and let Southeast Asia fall, there would follow a divisive and destructive debate in our country. . . .

"Third, our allies not just in Asia but throughout the world would conclude that our word was worth little or nothing. . . .

"Fourth, knowing what I did of the policies and actions of Moscow and Peking, I was as sure as a man could be that if we did not live up to our commitment in Southeast Asia and elsewhere, they would move to exploit the disarray in the United States and in the alliances of the Free World. . . .

"Finally, as we faced the implications of what we had done as a nation, I was sure that the United States . . . would return to a world role to prevent a full Communist takeover of Europe, Asia and the Middle East—*after* they had committed themselves."

On July 28, 1965, the escalating began in earnest. That evening, before the White House press corps, the President announced, "I have today ordered to Vietnam the Air Mobile Division and certain other forces which will raise our fighting strength from 75,000 to 125,000 men almost immediately." At the time, Mr. Johnson later wrote, U.S. military planners were thinking about assigning about 175,000 U.S. troops by the end of 1965 and another 100,000 in 1966.

But in early 1966, it was decided to raise U.S. troop levels in Vietnam to 385,000 by the end of 1966 and to 425,000 by the middle of 1967.

The war in Vietnam was very different from any other war that the U.S. had fought in, and most of the advantages lay, it often seemed, with the enemy. Mr. Johnson himself described the war this way: "The 'enemy' might be two or three divisions at one time, as at Khe Sanh, or two or three armed men sneaking into a village at night to murder the village chief. It was a war of subversion, terror, and assassination, of propaganda, economic disruption, and sabotage. It was a political war, an economic war, and a fighting war—all at the same time."

In addition to adding more men, the U.S. also escalated the war with its massive bombing. First, it was just a matter of bombing Dong Hoi and Van Linh. Then a few additional targets were added, and then many, many targets. By mid-

1965, the U.S. was flying 5,000 bombing sorties a month over North Vietnam. In the spring of 1966, fighter-bombers homed in on targets very close to Haiphong and Hanoi, key cities in the North. In April, B-52 bombers from Guam began raids for the first time.

There were, of course, some bombing pauses in the midst of the escalations. That included pauses of five days in May, 1965; thirty-seven days in late 1965 and early 1966; and six days in the spring of 1967. In all, there were eight pauses. From a propaganda standpoint, these pauses were helpful to Mr. Johnson's campaign to portray himself at home as a man of peace.

From day to day, the President's spirits rose and fell, depending on the way the war was going, the amount of publicity given to his opponents, the amount of publicity given to his own views. On many days, however, there was more darkness than light. The liberal intellectual community—Arthur Schlesinger, Jr.'s bailiwick—was almost completely lost to the administration. The nation's college campuses, the important ones especially, were angrily anti-Johnson. There were campus demonstrations, some of them violent. There was only one direction for the President's popularity generally: down. By November, 1967, the Gallup Poll rated his popularity at a lowly 38 per cent. American boys were dying by the hundreds each month, and the cost of the war—$27 billion for fiscal 1967 alone—was badly damaging the country's economy. Instead of a man of peace, as he wanted to portray himself, Mr. Johnson was being looked on more and more as a man of war, and an unpopular war, at that.

On the other hand, the military was increasingly restive. General Westmoreland, still pursuing a military victory against the resilient Asian Communist troops, wanted an increase in

U.S. troops—up to 680,000 men by June, 1968. What if the U.S. just stayed with the 470,000 men it had in Vietnam now, the President asked his general. It would mean, replied Westmoreland, that the U.S. would do little more than hold its own.

At one point, the President asked in frustration, "When we add divisions, can't the enemy add divisions? If so, where does it all end?"

The President was seeing more and more clearly where he stood. And he saw that he was in the middle, in a trap, caught between implacable civilian foes of the Vietnam War and the never-satisfied military, which always wants more men, more planes, more time to press for victory.

For once, Mr. Johnson could see nothing in his vast bag of political tricks that seemed to have any effect at all on the grievous problems at hand. Political power, he thought he had understood. Politics was an unruly pendulum, but if you understood its rhythms, if you could read its motions, then you knew about when to push and when to give in. You could control some of its momentum, and in a democratic society, that gave you at least the illusion, and perhaps the substance, of power. But now, every time he pushed, the pendulum seemed to push back.

The thought that Mr. Johnson might not run for another four-year term in 1968 struck most political observers as ridiculous. They believed that the President was too hopelessly addicted to power.

But the political pundits were overlooking two important factors in the President's situation. One was that after holding political power for nearly four decades, a man can find power beginning to lose its charm. The second factor was that a

President who uses great amounts of his power—as Mr. Johnson had done to conduct the Vietnam War—has less and less power to use as time goes by.

Realizing this, the President began, in March, 1968, to look for a graceful way to announce that he would not run again.

One of his observations about this time was how acutely depressed and frustrated the American people were with the Vietnam War, even more than the prior demonstrations had led him to believe. In late January, the Communists had launched a bold, quick, broadly coordinated attack throughout South Vietnam, and that attack, called the Tet offensive, had been something of a final straw for many Americans, the President observed. What really brought this home to him was a meeting on March 26 with his "Wise Men," as a group of his outside advisers on the war were called. The group included former Secretary of State Dean Acheson, former Undersecretary of State Ball, Gen. Omar Bradley, Ambassador Henry Cabot Lodge, and Gen. Maxwell Taylor, among others. In a word, their outlook on Vietnam was gloomy.

That surprised the President. He felt Tet, rather than a giant defeat, to be a series of events that had rallied the South Vietnamese people. In the long run, he looked on the January attacks as big pluses for the U.S. effort—not big minuses. But his Wise Men thought otherwise. "If they had been so deeply influenced by the reports of the Tet offensive, what must the average citizen in the country be thinking?" Mr. Johnson later wrote.

The agony and the impact of the war on American families was brought home acutely to Mr. Johnson the morning of March 31, a Sunday. That morning, he and Mrs. Johnson arose to greet their daughter Lynda at the south entrance to the White House. She had been flying all night, returning from California. There, she had said goodbye to her husband Chuck, who was headed for war duty in Vietnam. The war, the demonstrators, the loneliness—it all swept over the President's daughter in a river of tears. And Mr. Johnson felt powerless to comfort her.

It was a lonely time. The people, especially the brightest and the most outspoken, had taken another path; the President was no longer their leader in spirit. Where once they praised Caesar for his daring, his forcefulness, now they widely damned him for his heavy-handedness. Somehow, somewhere, large numbers of the American people had lost their respect for the flag, for the government, for the President.

At 9:01 P.M. on that March 31, Mr. Johnson took his cue from a network television director and began a speech to the nation from his Oval Office. He offered his view of the Tet offensive and noted that the U.S. planned to strengthen the South Vietnamese army. He said it was time to take new steps toward peace. He said that, tonight, he was ordering a halt to bombing above North Vietnam's 20th Parallel. He hoped North Vietnam would respond by entering into negotiations to end the war.

And then, at the end, the President said:

With America's sons in the fields far away, with America's future under challenge right here at home, with our hopes and the world's hopes for peace in the balance every day, I do not believe that I should devote an hour or a day of my time to any personal partisan causes or to any duties other than the awesome duties of this office—the Presidency of your country.

Accordingly, I shall not seek, and I will not accept the nomination of my party for another term as your President.

There. It was done. He had said it, and he meant it. Later that night, while talking with reporters, the President was asked how irrevocable his decision was. His answer: "Completely irrevocable."

For Lyndon Johnson, 1,886 days as President of the United States were all that he cared to serve. It was time, he felt, for another man to carry the load.

Chapter 14

HOMECOMING

The Vietnam War did not end during Lyndon Johnson's administration, but the bombing of North Vietnam did. And the bombing had to end before serious talks of ending the war could start.

The end of the bombing was part of a peace overture that Mr. Johnson undertook in October. By then, the nation was only a few weeks away from electing a new President, and Mr. Johnson's power was diminishing day by day. But this was, in those final days, a gesture, an important gesture, in the direction of peace.

On the last day of October, the 31st, about six o'clock in the evening, the President placed a conference call to three persons: Senator Hubert Humphrey, who was in Elizabeth, New Jersey. Former Vice-President Richard Nixon, who was at home in New York City. Governor George Wallace, who was in Norfolk, Virginia. The President told the three men, all candidates for his job in the November elections, that he was prepared to stop the bombing, believing that if he did, Hanoi was ready to negotiate.

He repeated that he had removed himself from the Presidential race back in March to devote all of his efforts toward achieving peace. With some hope that now North Vietnam would respond, he was pushing ahead, despite the nearness of the Presidential elections. His decision, Mr. Johnson said, was not a political one. He was not trying to bolster the candidacy of Senator Humphrey, the Democratic party candidate, and it was his hope that he could have the support of all three candidates.

"Let one man speak with a single voice to the Communist world and to the rest of the world," he said. Then he added, "Over and out. I'll be glad to have your comments."

Nixon had a question about the dangers of a ceasefire, if one developed. The President quickly reassured his questioner on that point, saying there would be no advantages permitted to the enemy.

Then the President told the trio on the phone that he would be announcing the bombing halt to the nation shortly. To this, Governor Wallace, the American party candidate, answered, "Mr. President, I just pray that everything you do works out fine, and I am praying for you."

Nixon, the Republican candidate, said, "We'll back you up. Thank you."

Humphrey said, "We'll back you, Mr. President."

Wallace added, "We'll back you, Mr. President."

At eight o'clock, a color film that had been made the past two days was run on national television. With a somber face—due in part to the fact that he was ill with a severe cold—the President outlined the developments of the past few days for the people of the United States. Then he said, "As a result of all these developments, I have now ordered that all air, naval, and artillery bombardment of North Vietnam cease as of 8 A.M., Washington time, Friday morning."

The United States had dropped more bombs on North Vietnam than it had dropped on Germany during World War II. What the costs were, it is impossible to calculate. For the U.S., the planes lost on the bombing raids totaled more than 900. The pilots of many of these planes had been killed or captured. As to the vast losses of the North Vietnamese, Americans will probably never know.

But perhaps all that was over. Perhaps now, there could be a political settlement during the coming Paris negotiations, and Vietnam could be at peace for the first time in generations.

Mr. Johnson wasn't making any promises. "What is required of us," he warned during his televised speech, "is a courage and a steadfastness, and a perseverance here at home, that will match that of our men who fight for us tonight in Vietnam." But he was hopeful.

Lady Bird had been up an hour on that final day in the White House—January 20, 1969—before Paul Glynn, the President's personal aide, knocked on the door to awaken Mr. Johnson. "It's seven o'clock, Mr. President," the Air Force sergeant called.

Outside the door to the Oval Office, as early as 7:30, all of Mr. Johnson's secretaries were at work, including Mary Rather, who had worked for Lyndon Johnson nearly thirty years. She was going home to Texas with the Johnsons; an ex-President still had letters to be typed.

The President-elect, Richard Nixon, and his family were due at 10:30, and about thirty minutes later, Mr. Johnson and his family would join the Nixons in a motorcade up Pennsylvania Avenue. A few minutes later, at the Capitol Building, Mr. Nixon would take the Presidential oath of office. With so little time left, Mr. Johnson knew he must hurry.

He had no last-minute bills to sign. His relationship with the Congress in those last hundred days had been a grave disappointment to him, a real sadness, since it had been in the U.S. Congress that Mr. Johnson had spent some of his most satisfying hours. But the war had poisoned congressional relations, and the defeats at the hands of Congress had tumbled out on the President. His hopes for a nuclear nonproliferation treaty, the appointment of a Chief Justice, his farm legislation, much of his proposed gun-control law—on all of it, Congress had balked.

The one circumstance that had given him great pleasure during those winding-down hours had been the launching of Apollo 7. The space mission was up safely; he had never lost his interest in the exploration of the skies.

But there were some other things of importance that Mr. Johnson wanted to do in the last few moments.

He wanted to sign a Presidential proclamation enlarging the national park system. There was still, even at that late hour, a question of how much land would be involved—whether it would be 7 million acres or much less—and that had to be settled with DeVier Pierson, one of the Johnson aides. Mr. Johnson also wanted to award the Medal of Freedom to five persons: Dean Rusk, Ambassador Averell Harriman, Secretary of Defense Clark Clifford, Presidential aide Walt Rostow and journalist William S. White. And there were a dozen vacancies on various national boards, commissions, and councils that the President wanted to fill.

In talking with Pierson, Mr. Johnson decided that 7

million acres was too much to add to the park service by Presidential decree. "A President shouldn't take this much land without the approval of Congress," Mr. Johnson said. So he signed a proclamation setting aside 300,000 acres, including a new national monument, Marble Canyon in Arizona.

The President instructed aide Harry Middleton to draw up the Medal of Honor citations, and while Mr. Johnson was dressing, aide Jim Jones brought in the citations and a folder of papers for the President's signature. He quickly signed all but two. "Hold these two letters until later," he said. "But make sure you bring them to my attention before we leave for the Capitol." Then Mr. Johnson turned to the White House barber, who gave him a fast trim.

The Nixons arrived precisely on schedule, and the two families, along with Hubert Humphrey, Vice-President-elect Spiro Agnew and their families, and several congressional leaders, visited briefly in the Red Room.

Mr. Johnson, in a light-hearted mood, told a story about a Texas friend he had once visited. "Let me tell you a story," Mr. Johnson had said to his friend, and the man, who had probably heard the President's stories before, asked, "OK, but how long will it take?"

"Well, Dick," the President said, eyes twinkling, "I don't want to be like that fellow, but I'm curious. How long will your inaugural address take?"

Mr. Nixon replied that the speech ran just over two thousand words and that it should take about twenty minutes.

Before leaving for his final Presidential procession through Washington, Mr. Johnson asked for the two letters that Jim Jones was holding. They were personal notes, both of them. They were addressed to Mr. Johnson's sons-in-law, Chuck Robb and Pat Nugent. They were U.S. soldiers, stationed in Vietnam. Those letters were the last two documents that Mr. Johnson signed while President.

At 11:05, the motorcade left the north portico of the White House. Not long after, Richard Nixon was taking the oath of office. As Mr. Nixon concluded the words, ". . . So help me God," the Presidential duties of Lyndon Johnson came to an end.

That night, aboard *Air Force One*, he left for Texas.

EPILOGUE

Lyndon Baines Johnson died on January 22, 1973, of a heart attack. It was a Monday afternoon, and he was at the LBJ Ranch, his home since leaving Washington. Before losing consciousness, Mr. Johnson was able to alert a Secret Service man, who was at his side within moments. But it was too late. The ex-President, a man literally addicted to hard work, had been felled by a disease that often afflicts those who have hurried through life.

The body of the late President was flown to Washington for honors and funeral ceremonies, and then once more, for the final time, Mr. Johnson came flying home on *Air Force One*. That memorable trip, on a bitingly cold winter day, was made on January 25.

On the final day of his life, typically, the sixty-four-year-old Mr. Johnson had been busy at many things. One of the matters that had concerned him was a visit by Prime Minister Golda Meir of Israel to the LBJ School of Public Affairs at the University of Texas in Austin. Mr. Johnson wanted students at the LBJ School to be exposed, as he put it, to "practical practicing politicians—people who really know what public service is all about—and not just a bunch of professors."

He was proud of the LBJ School of Public Affairs and of the Lyndon Baines Johnson Library, both built on a fourteen-acre knoll on the Austin campus. The library was eight stories tall, and it contained the 31 million pages of documents, ranging across Mr. Johnson's thirty-seven years in public life. One of the great thrills for the ex-President—and for any museum visitor—was to stand in the museum's Great Hall and look up at the four stories of storage boxes, each carrying a small gold replica of the Presidential seal, that were visible through glass walls.

The President had some happy moments on that final day. He was pleased that his son-in-law Patrick Nugent was planning to rejoin the family broadcasting business in Austin. It was no secret that Mr. Johnson wanted his son-in-law to run the business someday.

Another source of pleasure to Mr. Johnson in those final hours was the impending visit of an Atlanta industrialist, J. B. Fuqua, who had become a close friend in the past two or three years. Mr. Johnson claimed that there aren't many important people who will drop in on a man who has retired from public life and is out of the national spotlight.

That wasn't really true, of course. The decision to stay out of the public eye, out of both Texas and national politics, had been Mr. Johnson's decision, and not that of his friends and supporters. He had announced before leaving the White House that he planned to retire to the LBJ Ranch and read, write, and loaf. But knowing Lyndon Johnson as well as many of his close friends did, most of them laughed. That was just another of Mr. Johnson's stories, they said.

But Mr. Johnson had meant what he said. He had been a

public man for thirty-seven years, and that was enough. A man didn't live forever. He deserved some time for himself, for his family, for his grandchildren. During all those years of public service, Washington had really been home, but he had come back to Texas at every opportunity, and now that he was back, he had no intention of being enticed away again.

They buried him in the family plot, close to the LBJ Ranch headquarters, beneath a spreading live oak tree. On summer days, the buzzards spiral in the Hill Country skies. A few feet away, the Pedernales River slips quietly by.

This was once, and will always be, Presidential Country.

BIBLIOGRAPHY

(° Indicates books which were especially helpful in the preparation of this book.)

° ARMRINE, MICHAEL, *This Awesome Challenge: The 100 Days of Lyndon Johnson.* New York, G. P. Putnam's Sons, 1964.

ANDERSON, PATRICK, *The President's Men.* New York, Doubleday & Co., 1968.

BAKER, LEONARD, *The Johnson Eclipse: A President's Vice-Presidency.* New York, The Macmillan Co., 1966.

° BELL, JACK, *The Johnson Treatment: How Lyndon B. Johnson Took Over the Presidency and Made It His Own.* New York, Harper & Row, 1965.

° BISHOP, JIM, *A Day in the Life of President Johnson.* New York, Random House, 1967.

BUCHWALD, ART, *. . . and then I told the President. The Secret Papers of Art Buchwald.* New York, G. P. Putnam's Sons, 1964, 1965.

° BURNS, JAMES MAC GREGOR, ed., *To Heal and to Build: The Programs of Lyndon B. Johnson.* New York, McGraw-Hill, 1968.

CAIDIN, MARTIN, and HYMOFF, EDWARD, *The Mission.* Philadelphia, J. B. Lippincott, 1964.

° CARPENTER, LIZ, *Ruffles and Flourishes.* New York, Doubleday & Co., 1970.

° CHRISTIAN, GEORGE, *The President Steps Down* (original title—*LBJ: The Last 100 Days*). New York, The Macmillan Co., 1970.

CLEMENS, CYRIL, *Mark Twain and Lyndon B. Johnson.* Kirkwood, Miss. *Mark Twain Journal,* 1967.

CURTIS, RICHARD, and WELLS, MAGGIE, *Not Exactly a Crime: Our Vice-Presidents from Adams to Agnew.* New York, Dial Press, 1972.

DAVIE, MICHAEL, *LBJ: A Foreign Observer's Viewpoint.* New York, Duell, Sloan, and Pearce, 1966.

DEAKIN, JAMES. *Lyndon Johnson's Credibility Gap.* Washington, Public Affairs Press, 1968.

DESTLER, I. M., *Presidents, Bureaucrats, and Foreign Policy.* Princeton, Princeton University Press, 1972.

DRUKS, HERBERT, *From Truman Through Johnson: A Documentary History.* New York, Robert Speller & Sons, 1971.

DUGGER, RONNIE, *Johnson: From Poverty to Power.* New York, N. W. Norton & Co., 1968.

° EVANS, ROWLAND, and NOVAK, ROBERT, *Lyndon B. Johnson: The Exercise of Power.* New York, The New American Library, 1966.

GEYELIN, PHILIP L., *Lyndon B. Johnson and the World.* New York, Praeger Publishers, 1966.

° GOLDMAN, ERIC F., *The Tragedy of Lyndon Johnson.* New York, Alfred A. Knopf, 1968.

GRAFF, HENRY F., *The Tuesday Cabinet.* Englewood Cliffs, N.J., Prentice-Hall, 1970.

° HALBERSTAM, DAVID, *The Best and the Brightest.* New York, Random House, 1972.

HALEY, J. EVETTS, *A Texan Looks at Lyndon.* Texas, Palo Duro Press, 1964.

° HEREN, LOUIS, *No Hail, No Farewell.* New York, Harper & Row, 1970.

HYMAN, SIDNEY, *Politics of Consensus.* New York, Random House, 1968.

° JOHNSON, CLAUDIA A., *White House Diary.* New York, Holt, Rinehart and Winston, 1970.

JOHNSON, LYNDON BAINES, *Choices We Face*. New York, Bantam Books, 1969.

———, *My Hope for America*. New York, Random House, 1964.

———, "My Political Philosophy," *The Texas Quarterly*, Vol. 1, No. 4, Winter 1958, pp. 17–22.

———, *No Retreat from Tomorrow*. New York, Doubleday & Co., 1968.

———, *Public Papers of the Presidents of the United States: Lyndon B. Johnson, 1963–1964, 1965, 1966*. Washington, D.C., Government Printing Office.

———, *The Quotable LBJ*, edited by Sarah H. Hayes. New York, Grosset & Dunlap, 1968.

———, *This America*. New York, Random House, 1966.

° ———, *A Time for Action: A Selection from the Speeches and Writings of Lyndon B. Johnson, 1953–1964*. New York, Atheneum, 1964.

° ———, *The Vantage Point: Perspectives of the Presidency, 1963–1969*. New York, Holt, Rinehart and Winston, 1971.

° JOHNSON, REBEKAH BAINES, *A Family Album*. New York, McGraw-Hill, 1965.

———, *The Johnsons, Descendants of John Johnson, a Revolutionary Soldier of Georgia: A Genealogical History*, privately printed, October 11, 1956.

° JOHNSON, SAM HOUSTON, *My Brother Lyndon*. New York, Cowles Book Co., 1969.

° JUDAH, CHARLES, and SMITH, G. W., *Unchosen*. New York, Coward-McCann, 1962, pp. 303–332.

KITTLER, GLENN D., *Hail to the Chief: The Inauguration Days of Our Presidents*. Philadelphia, Chilton Book Co., 1965, pp. 219–231.

KLUCKHOHN, FRANK L., *Lyndon's Legacy: A Candid Look at the President's Policy Makers*. Old Greenwich, Conn., The Devin-Adair Co., 1964.

LAWRENCE, BILL, *Six Presidents, Too Many Wars*. Dallas, Cokesbury Press, 1972.

LEIGHTON, FRANCES SPATZ, ed., *The Johnson Wit.* New York, Citadel Press, 1965.

LINCOLN, EVELYN, *Kennedy and Johnson.* New York, Holt, Rinehart and Winston, 1968.

MC PHERSON, HARRY, *A Political Education.* Boston, Little, Brown & Co., 1972.

MAGUIRE, JACK, ed., *A President's Country: A Guide to the Hill Country of Texas.* Austin, Tex., The Alcade Press, 1964.

MANCHESTER, WILLIAM, *Death of a President.* New York, Harper & Row, 1967.

° MOONEY, BOOTH, *Lyndon Johnson Story,* rev. ed. New York, Farrar, Straus & Giroux, 1964.

° NEWLON, CLARKE, *LBJ: The Man From Johnson City.* New York, Dodd, Mead & Co., 1964.

OPOTOWSKY, STAN, *Kennedy Government.* New York, E. P. Dutton, 1961, pp. 38–48.

° POOL, WILLIAM C., CRADDOCK, EMMIE, and CONRAD, DAVID E., *Lyndon Baines Johnson: The Formative Years.* San Marcos, Tex., Southwest Texas State College Press, 1965.

° PORTERFIELD, BILL, *LBJ Country.* New York, Doubleday & Co., 1965.

PROVENCE, HARRY, *Lyndon B. Johnson: A Biography.* New York, Fleet Press Corp., 1964.

ROBERTS, CHARLES, *LBJ's Inner Circle.* New York, Delacorte Press, 1965.

ROSENBLUM, SIG, and ANTIN, CHARLES, eds., *LBJ Lampooned: Cartoon Criticism of Lyndon B. Johnson.* New York, Cobble Hill Press, 1968.

ROWEN, HOBART, *The Free Enterprisers: Kennedy, Johnson, and the Business Establishment.* New York, G. P. Putnam's Sons, 1964.

SALOMA, JOHN S., III, and SONTAG, FREDERICK H., *Parties: The Real Opportunity for Effective Citizen Politics.* New York, Alfred A. Knopf, 1972.

SEVAREID, ERIC, ed., *Candidates 1960.* New York, Basic Books, 1959, pp. 280–321.

SHERRILL, ROBERT, *The Accidental President*. New York, Grossman Publishers, 1967.

° SIDEY, HUGH, *A Very Personal Presidency: Lyndon Johnson in the White House*. New York, Atheneum, 1968.

° SINGER, K. D. and SHERROD, J., *Lyndon Baines Johnson, Man of Reason*. Minneapolis, T. S. Denison & Co., 1964.

SMITH, TIMOTHY G., ed., *Merriman Smith's Book of Presidents. A White House Memoir*. New York, N. W. Norton & Co., 1971.

° STEINBERG, ALFRED, *Sam Johnson's Boy: A Close-up of the President from Texas*. New York, The Macmillan Co., 1968.

SUNDQUIST, JAMES L., *Politics and Policy: The Eisenhower, Kennedy and Johnson Years*. Washington, Brookings Institute, 1968.

Tributes to the President and Mrs. Lyndon B. Johnson in the Congress of the United States, U. S. 91st Congress, 1st session. Washington, D.C., Government Printing Office, 1969.

U. S. PRESIDENT, 1963–68, *President Johnson's Design for a "Great Society"; Texts of President Johnson's Messages to the 89th Congress*. Washington, D.C., Congressional Quarterly Service, 1965.

WHITE, THEODORE, *The Making of the President 1960*. New York, Atheneum, 1961.

———, *The Making of the President, 1964*. New York, Atheneum, 1965.

WHITE, WILLIAM S., *The Professional: Lyndon B. Johnson*. Boston, Houghton Mifflin, Co., 1964.

———, *Responsibles: How Five American Leaders Coped with Crisis*. New York, Harper & Row, 1971.

WICKER, TOM, *JFK and LBJ: The Influence of Personality Upon Politics*. New York, William Morrow & Co., 1968.

ZEIGER, HENRY A., *Lyndon B. Johnson: Man and President*. New York, Popular Library, 1963.

INDEX

ABOUT THE AUTHOR

Dudley Lynch is a free-lance writer-correspondent, covering the North Texas area for national magazines and newspapers. His articles have appeared in *Newsweek*, *Business Week*, the *Christian Science Monitor*, *The New York Times*, *Southern Voices*, the *Texas Observer*, and many other publications.

Born in Tennessee, Mr. Lynch is a graduate of Eastern New Mexico University, with a master's degree in journalism from the University of Texas. With his wife and two young daughters he lives in Garland, Texas, where he enjoys canoeing on the Brazos River in a redwood and fiber glass canoe he built himself.